THE

LIFE OF THE SAVIOUR.

BY

HENRY WARE, Jr.

SEVENTH EDITION.

BOSTON:
AMERICAN UNITARIAN ASSOCIATION.
1873.

Entered according to Act of Congress, in the year 1868, by the
AMERICAN UNITARIAN ASSOCIATION,
in the Clerk's Office of the District Court of the District of Massachusetts.

UNIVERSITY PRESS: WELCH, BIGELOW, & Co.,
CAMBRIDGE.

EDITORIAL NOTE

TO THE SIXTH EDITION.

THIS volume is reprinted at the request of the Ladies' Commission on Sunday-School Books, after an interval of more than twenty years since the last (the 5th) edition was issued, during most of which period it has been out of print. These twenty years have been marked by more than usual activity of thought upon this great subject, and it was at first proposed to have the book revised, so that it might be enriched and perhaps amended by what later scholarship has contributed towards the better understanding of the Life of Christ. But it has seemed on the whole unnecessary to do this. The volume is the interpretation of the lessons of our Saviour's life and teachings, given by one who eminently possessed the qualifications for such a task; and the repeated call for it has sufficiently proved that it has earned a permanent place among the many similar works to which such study has led, and which the Christian faith accepts as helps and guides.

BOSTON, JAN. 1, 1868.

PREFACE.

THE principles adopted in the arrangement of the present history are sufficiently explained in the course of the work. That they will be universally satisfactory is not to be expected. The essential difficulties of constructing a harmony of the evangelical historians are such as to forbid the expectation. But I cannot persuade myself that I am mistaken in thinking that the system here adopted has greater probabilities in its favor than any other which has been suggested. A full statement of the reasons on which it rests is incompatible with the limits of the work.

I would suggest to my readers, that they will find the instruction and interest of the volume greatly increased by carefully examining in connection with it the passages referred to at the bottom of the pages. Indeed, much of the pertinency of many remarks and illustrations will be otherwise unperceived. The most convenient mode of doing this will be by using the *Harmony of the Gospels*, mentioned in the note on the 44th page.

I am aware that many things will be found unexplained which need explanation, and that defects and omissions will be perceived by others which have escaped my own observation. But I hope that, notwithstanding these, I have not altogether failed in the attempt to unfold to young minds some of the interesting points in our Saviour's history, and to excite in them a desire to be more intimately instructed in its wonderful and beautiful records. It would be a great happiness to believe that I had aided in bringing any to a true admiration and faithful love of our blessed Lord.

CAMBRIDGE, JAN. 4, 1833.

NOTE

TO THE SECOND EDITION.

I HAVE availed myself of the call for another edition of this work to make several additions and some changes in various parts of the volume. None of these are of much moment, except an additional chapter at the close of the work, and the exclusion, from the first chapters, of what was drawn from the apocryphal histories. This change is made at the suggestion of several friends, and I trust will be disapproved by none.

CAMBRIDGE, OCT. 8, 1833.

CONTENTS.

CHAPTER VIII.

CHAPTER IX.

CHAPTER X.

CHAPTER XI.

CHAPTER XII.

CHAPTER XIII.

CHAPTER XIV.

CHAPTER XV.

CHAPTER XVI.

CHAPTER XVII.

CHAPTER XVIII.

CHAPTER XIX.

CHAPTER XX.

CHAPTER XXI.

CHAPTER XXII.

CHAPTER XXIII.

THE

LIFE OF THE SAVIOUR.

CHAPTER I.

THE PARENTAGE AND DESCENT OF JESUS.

IT is usual to begin the life of a distinguished person with an account of his family and parents. Sometimes the line of descent is traced back generation after generation, and it is boasted from what celebrated ancestors he sprung. Sometimes it is acknowledged that he was of obscure origin, and has been the founder of his own fame and family. In either case it is thought that the circumstance is honorable to him. In the first, he derives splendor and dignity from the great men from whom he descended. In the second, what can be more creditable than to have risen from nothing, by his own industry and talents, to an equality with those whose natural advantages were superior?

Two of the Evangelists who have written the history of our Saviour begin their account of him in this way. They give the genealogy of his family, and show his descent from the kings of Judah. His immediate parentage was obscure. Joseph and Mary were persons of no note, and he was born to the condition of humble life. But his remote ancestors were of the royal family, and through them his lineage went back to the distinguished fathers and founders of the nation; through David, the great king, to Abraham, the chief progenitor, and to Seth, the son of Adam, the first man, who was the son of God. Thus, regarded only in a human point of view, this wonderful person united in himself the two circumstances mentioned above, to which biographers draw attention, that they may exalt the persons they celebrate. He was of poor and humble parents, yet rose to eminence above all persons of his age and country. He was also of honorable ancestors, belonging to the chief family of the nation, ennobled by descent from the greatest names in human history, and able to trace his lineage up to the first man, who was the immediate creation of God.

The Evangelists point out another remarkable distinction of our Lord's descent. It is capable of being traced to its original stock through both parents. The family of Joseph and the family of Mary both run back till they meet in David, and thence proceed in a common line to Abraham.

Matthew i. 1. Luke iii. 13.

This renders his descent doubly illustrious. The genealogy of Joseph is given by Matthew, and that of Mary by Luke.

Besides the circumstances already mentioned, which give an interest to this subject, it is to be considered, that this was amongst the Jews a matter of extreme importance. Every family kept its genealogical register, and knew the list of its ancestry from the earliest day. This was necessary on account of some peculiar requisitions in their law respecting property and inheritance; which required evidence of the tribe and family to which every individual belonged. There was a further reason which made it a matter of interest. The promised and expected Messiah — that great prince and deliverer, of whom the prophets had so rapturously spoken, and on whose coming the hopes and glory of the nation were suspended — was to be of the tribe of Judah and the family of David. It was important therefore to be able to trace the descent of every individual who should claim to be this person. Hence the records of that family, and of every branch of that family, would be kept with the most jealous care, in order that it might be proved, when the Messiah came, that he was in truth of the right stock. There can be no doubt that the descent of Jesus was carefully searched into by those who questioned or opposed his claims; and as they do not appear to have objected to him on this ground, there can be no doubt that the tables of his genealogy, published by his disciples, were faithful copies from the family and public registers; though we know too little of the Jewish method of keeping those tables to be able to clear away all difficulty from the subject.

We must not be surprised, then, that the Evangelists have given so much room to this subject. It was necessary to prove that their Master was the son of David; for otherwise he could not be the Messiah. And it is curious to observe how, even on a point in which worldly ambition so often boasts of superiority, our blessed Lord is placed far above the illustrious names of human history. Where are the potentates, lords, and princes, in all their pride of birth, who can look back on so honorable and ancient a line of progenitors; — passing on, through nobles and kings, lawgivers and prophets, beyond the date of all other records, till it ends in the name of the first man, and God the Universal Parent?

Of Joseph, the husband of our Lord's mother, and his reputed father, we know very little. He is said to have been an upright and just man; and the little which is told of him in the New Testament proves him to have been such. There is a tradition that he was married to Mary when quite advanced in life, while she was but fourteen years of age. Hence it is, that in all the pictures of the holy family he is painted as an aged man, while the Virgin is represented as young enough to be his granddaughter. But there is no good reason for supposing the tradition to be true. We can only say, that we know nothing of his age, and that it is a matter of no consequence. It is more important to remember, that he exercised a mechanical trade, and depended on the work of his hands for a livelihood. He was a carpenter; and it is extremely probable, as the Jews called Jesus also a carpenter, that he, together with the sons of Joseph, learned that trade and worked at it. This will explain how it happened that his brothers did not believe on him. They had always seen him living amongst them like one of themselves, and they could not readily understand how their companion and equal in sports and labors should be the Son of God.

Of Mary, our Lord's mother, we know something more, though much less than we should be glad to know of so interesting a being. It is not strange that men have been eager to learn all that concerned her; that in superstitious ages they have listened to any tales invented to her honor, and have contrived how they might show her the greatest respect. This has been carried so far that multitudes of Christians have made her an object of worship; and by images and pictures, by processions and offerings and hymns, have expressed their veneration for the mother of their Lord, and the natural interest they feel in her character and fortunes. In one gallery in Florence there are two hundred and forty pictures of the Virgin, mostly from the hands of the first masters. Many churches have been erected to her honor, and thousands of altars, at which she is adored, are hung round with the offerings of grateful and devoted worshippers. It is sad to witness such a diversion of good feelings from the homage of God to the adoration of a human being. Yet, perhaps, it is true that we Protestants do not allow ourselves to indulge the feelings which are rightfully due to the mother of Jesus, because we have seen them perverted. We should learn to be more just; and this we may be without becoming superstitious.

We know nothing certain of Mary, until an angel appeared to her at Nazareth, and saluted her with those memorable words, "Hail, thou that art highly favored! The Lord is with thee! Blessed art thou among women!" One may easily imagine what her feelings of surprise and wonder would be. The Evangelist tells us, that she was troubled at the saying of the angel, and waited anxiously to learn what might be his message. The angel went on; told her that God had

Luke i. 26.

designed for her the great honor of being mother to the Messiah; that she should call his name Jesus (that is, Saviour), because he should "save his people from their sins"; and that, because of his miraculous birth, he should be called the Son of God. Mary received this astonishing message with simplicity and meekness. "Behold," said she, "the handmaid of the Lord; be it unto me according to thy word."

We may imagine the agitation and ecstasy of feeling which filled the breast of this poor and humble maiden. At a time when all Israel was looking out earnestly for the coming of the great deliverer, and all the women of the land, the high and the noble, were hoping that some son of theirs should prove the Messiah, this obscure woman is suddenly assured by a messenger from heaven that she is to be the favored person,—that the honorable ladies of Jerusalem and the palaces of the chief rulers have been passed by, and a lowly dwelling of a distant country village is selected as the home of the future prince. In the excitement of such a moment, overwhelmed by feelings which are not to be described, and which yet must long to find vent and sympathy, whither should she go? There was her cousin Elizabeth, who a few months before had been visited with a similar message, and whose son was to be an extraordinary prophet. She, said Mary to herself, will sympathize with me. Accordingly, as Luke tells us, she arose in haste, and went into the city in which Elizabeth resided. What a meeting was that, between two women who knew themselves about to be the mothers of the great prophets for whom the nation was anxiously looking! No wonder that it has been a favorite subject with religious painters. And what must have been the delight of their intercourse during the three months that Mary's visit continued! Probably they did not know, they could not know, they could not guess, all the wonderful and gracious consequences to flow upon their nation and on mankind from the ministry of their unborn sons; but they could gather enough from the magnificent language of the Prophets, whose writings they undoubtedly read and pondered together, to excite the most exalted anticipations, and cherish a spirit of the highest religious rejoicing.

Having made a visit of about three months, Mary returned to her home, and shortly afterwards Elizabeth gave birth to a son. This was John the Baptist.

CHAPTER II.

HIS BIRTH AND CHILDHOOD.

At the time of which we are writing, the Jewish nation had fallen from its ancient power and greatness. It was no longer the same prosperous people that it had been in the days of David and Solomon. Its independence was gone. The great Roman nation, which had extended its wars and conquests over a large portion of the known world, had subdued Judæa also, and reduced it to the condition of a dependent kingdom. Herod, a native prince, was permitted to occupy the throne; but he was obliged to govern according to the pleasure of the Roman Emperor, and the land may be regarded as having become virtually a province of Rome, though it was not yet such in form.

It is a mark of this subjection to the Roman power, that when Augustus issued his decree for taking the census of the Empire, Judæa was included. In the common translation of Luke's Gospel, this is spoken of as a *taxation;* but it was properly only an enumeration of the inhabitants, whose names were to be registered by proper officers. It is said, too, to be the census of "all the world"; by which is to be understood the Roman world, or empire; though many suppose that only the Jewish world or country is intended. In executing this decree in Palestine, it was ordered that the names of the people should be taken according to their tribes and families, — probably because the Jews were accustomed to reckon by families rather than by place of abode. Accordingly all went to be enrolled or registered, "every one in his own city." Now Joseph and Mary, as we have seen, were of the tribe of Judah and the family of David. But they were residing at Nazareth, in the tribe of Zebulon. They were therefore compelled, in obedience to this law, to travel from home, nearly a hundred miles, to the town of Bethlehem. This town was called *the city of David*, because David and his ancestors were born there. Hence Boaz, David's great-grandfather, called it the "city of his people." It was the ancestral home of both Joseph and Mary. Thither therefore they repaired. At the same time, all descendants of the same family, in whatever part of the country they might reside, collected together in the same city. It was not a large town, and was soon filled to overflowing by the people who were thus brought together.

Luke ii. 2.

It is not therefore surprising, that, when Joseph and Mary arrived from Galilee, they found all the rooms at the inn occupied, and were obliged to take up with a lodging in the stable. The inhabitants of Bethlehem to the present day point out a cave as the place in which the Saviour was born. It has been so regarded from time immemorial, and a church has stood over it for ages to mark the spot. Many, however, think the supposition absurd. But, whether it be so or not, into a stable were these weary travellers obliged to go for lodging; and there was born the King of the Jews, the Saviour of the world. Little did the multitude assembled there think, when they heard that a poor woman in the stable had given birth to a son, that that son was to be the most illustrious of all that were born of woman. Little did the pious men and women who were waiting for the salvation of Israel, and the ambitious and impatient rulers and people whose eyes were straining after their promised prince, — little did they fancy that he was already among them in that humble place. They were looking for him in the high places of the earth, and in the families of the great. They thought he would come with a sign from heaven, with pomp and power. But there he was, lying in a manger, unnoticed as any common child.

The superstitious of later times have delighted

to connect marvels with this event, as if not satisfied with the simple and unostentatious manner in which Providence had been pleased to conduct it. They have given a celestial lustre to the body of the new-born babe, and represented it, in their pictures, as splendidly shining by its own light. They have said that the very cattle which stood by fell upon their knees to acknowledge the heaven-descended child; and multitudes still believe, that at midnight, on the anniversary of the nativity, the cattle everywhere kneel in their stalls to commemorate the Redeemer's birth. But all this is the imagination of man. In no such puerile way did Providence testify to the greatness of the infant prophet. The wonders which God wrought were of a higher and more significant character.

It is customary among men to announce the birth of a prince by formal messages to other princes, in order to receive their congratulations, and to proclaim it in form to the people over whom he is to reign. The Evangelist has recorded something of this kind on the present occasion. Not indeed a message to princes, or a proclamation to the nation; but something far more beautiful, and more consonant to the nature of the new kingdom of the Messiah. In the still midnight, while the shepherds of Bethlehem were watching their flocks in the fields, a light burst *upon them from the heavens, and the angel of* the Lord, as an ambassador from God, appeared before them. He announced to them the birth of the Messiah, and was immediately joined by a multitude of voices, singing that delightful anthem, "Glory to God in the highest, and on earth peace, good-will towards men." The shepherds went to Bethlehem, and found the child as the angel had said; and Mary, strongly affected by this new proof that she was mother of the Messiah, "kept all these things and pondered them in her heart."

After forty days had passed, the time arrived when she must present herself with her child at the temple, and make the offerings which the law required. It being her first child, there was a double ceremony to be performed Forty days after the birth of all children, the mother was bound to appear at the temple with the sacrifice of a lamb for a burnt-offering, and a turtle dove or a young pigeon for a sin-offering. Those who could not afford to bring a lamb were allowed to offer a pigeon or turtle dove as a substitute; and it is an evidence of the humble station of Mary, that she brought two turtle doves, — the offering which was permitted to the poor. Besides this, which was required at the birth of every child, in the case of the first-born son there was an extraordinary ceremony to be passed through. In order to keep alive a solemn memory of the providence which delivered the nation from Egypt by the death of the Egyptian first-born, the law required that every first-born male, of man and of beast, should be sacred to the Lord ; — the beast to be sacrificed, and the child to be redeemed. This redemption consisted in paying to the priest, for the service of the temple, five shekels ; * a sum equal to about two dollars seventy - eight cents. Mary therefore must redeem her child. Accordingly, having presented her humble sacrifice, she proceeded " to do for him," as the Evangelist says, " after the custom of the law " ; that is, to present him to the Lord, and pay the price of his redemption. Here she was called to another scene which honored her son, and tried and delighted her own feelings.

There was an aged man in Jerusalem by the name of Simeon, a devout and religious person, whose mind was filled with an earnest longing for the coming of the Messiah and the consolation of Israel. And he had been favored with the assurance that he should not die until his desire had been accomplished. This venerable saint had come into the temple just at the moment when the parents of Jesus had brought their first-born to the altar; and, being assured that this was the child for whose coming he had been waiting,

* Numbers xviii. 15, 16.

he took it in his arms, and, giving utterance to his holy delight, blessed God and said: "Lord, now lettest thou thy servant depart in peace! for mine eyes have seen thy salvation." He added a prophecy of the greatness and the offices of the child. This was not all. Scarcely had he ended, when the wondering parents were astonished by the entrance of another ancient person, a prophetess named Anna, who dwelt continually in the temple, occupied in offices of religion. On seeing the child, she broke out in thanksgiving to God, and spake of him to all who looked for redemption in Jerusalem. By such circumstances was the faith of the parents confirmed.

Another event is recorded by Matthew, by which the nativity was honored and proclaimed. Certain Magi, philosophers from some Eastern country (he does not say what), having seen an unusual star, and believing, as was a common idea in ancient times, that it intimated the birth of an extraordinary person, followed it till they arrived at Jerusalem. There had long prevailed an expectation in that part of the world, that a great prince should arise in Judæa and obtain the empire of the world. These philosophers did not doubt that this star was sent to proclaim his coming. And they accordingly inquired on their arrival, "Where is he that is born king of the

Matthew ii.

Jews? for we have seen his star in the east, and are come to worship him." In former days the word *worship* expressed the homage paid to princes and great men, as well as that paid to God. They seem to have made this inquiry of King Herod himself; as was very natural they should do, for they would readily suppose that the new-born prince would be one of the royal family. But no; Herod knew nothing of it; and not only so, but he was greatly troubled to hear it. He was aware that the Messiah was expected; he thought that this might be he, and he feared therefore for his own power and authority. He seems to have resolved at once on the course to be taken. He accordingly summoned a meeting of the chief priests and scribes. This was probably the great council of the Sanhedrim. He inquired of them at what place the Messiah was to be born. They referred him to a passage of the prophet Micah [v. 2.], in proof that he would be born at Bethlehem of Judæa. To Bethlehem therefore he sent the inquiring strangers; directing them to return to him when they had found the child, that he too might go and show him honor.

To Bethlehem accordingly they went. There they prostrated themselves in the Oriental fashion before the infant, and, agreeably to the customs of the world, laid before him their presents of gold, frankincense, and myrrh. But they were not permitted to return to Herod, for that crafty tyrant meditated the death of the infant. They were directed in a dream to avoid Jerusalem, and return to their country by another route. At the same time Joseph was warned in a dream of the danger to which the infant was exposed, and directed to quit the country, and take refuge in Egypt. Thus he escaped the murderous jealousy of the king. But Herod was exceedingly exasperated ; and, resolving to be sure that the dreaded infant did not escape, caused all the infant children of about the age of Jesus, in Bethlehem and its neighborhood, to be put to death. This cruel act has seemed to some persons too savage to be true. But Herod was a monster of cruelty, and is well known to have done other acts as horrible as this.

But it was in vain that the angry king raged against the anointed of the Lord. He could not thwart the purposes of God. The infant whom he thought to destroy was destined to accomplish great purposes in the kingdom of Divine grace, and therefore a way was made for his escape from the danger which threatened him. While Herod pleased himself with thinking him slain, he was safely conveyed into Egypt. His parents departed with him by night, and travelled over a portion of the desert which the Israelites crossed under the guidance of Moses. The distance was not far from two hundred miles, — a weary and painful journey for a young mother with an infant babe. It must have been, also, no small trial to her faith. Is it thus, she might say, that the visions of the night, the promise of the angel, and the prophecies in the temple, are to be accomplished? Are we thus to be compelled to flee for our lives, to endure the perils of the desert, and the want and anxiety of a strange land? Would God thus deal with his Messiah? Is it not possible that, after all, I have been deceived? We may conceive that moments of despondency like this must have sometimes beset her. Her case was not unlike that of Abraham, when travelling for three days to sacrifice his only son Isaac, — that son to whom God had made great promises, which it seemed as if his death must defeat. But as Abraham, though he might have been amazed and have experienced momentary misgivings, yet went steadfastly on, unshaken in his faith; so Mary, however strange she might think this dispensation, and however inconsistent with the promises made to the young Messiah, undoubtedly kept her faith strong, and trusted in the Lord.

Of their residence in Egypt we know nothing, except that it continued till the death of Herod, which took place within three years. Upon the tidings of that event reaching him, Joseph felt that all danger was over. He therefore returned to his own country, and took up his abode once more at Nazareth. This was a small town in Galilee, about seventy-five miles north of Jerusalem. Its inhabitants were not in very good repute through the country, and such a prejudice existed against the place, that "a Nazarene" had become a term of contempt. It is important to remark this, because we see frequent intimations of it in the course of our Lord's subsequent life; and the Evangelist Matthew, when he would say that the prophecies concerning the Messiah's humiliation were fulfilled, sums them all up in one word, "He shall be called a Nazarene." We know too that when Nathaniel first heard of Jesus, he thought it impossible he should be the Messiah, because he came from this despised place. "Can any good thing," said he, "come out of Nazareth?"

It was undoubtedly a part of the plan of Providence to draw the Saviour from humble human circumstances, in order to render his Divine authority the more conspicuous and unquestionable. It was thus made to appear that his words of wisdom could not have been learned from man, and that he must have been from God. He probably received little or no education during his early years; for the Jews asked, "How knoweth this man letters, having never learned?" Schools and instruction were not then universal as they are now, and Joseph was probably too poor to afford to his children a privilege which could be purchased only by the rich.

This however is not stated in the New Testament. There is far less there respecting his early years than we should be glad to find. We only read in general terms, that "the child grew and waxed strong in spirit, filled with wisdom; and the grace of God was upon him. He increased in wisdom and stature, and in favor with God and man." Of particular incidents only one is recorded. When he was twelve years of age, he accompanied his parents to Jerusalem, when they went up, in obedience to the law, to keep the passover. The seven days of the feast were over, and they set out on their return. They had proceeded a whole day's journey before they discovered that Jesus was not accompanying them. We may easily understand how this could happen, when we remember, that the law commanded all the men, from all parts of the land, to go up and keep this feast at Jerusalem. Consequently, there must have been great throngs on the road, both in going and returning. The people naturally travelled in parties. The inhabitants of a village made one company. Families, in all their branches,

Luke ii. 40.

went together. The parents of Jesus, therefore, being in company with a vast number of relatives and neighbors, did not think it strange that they did not see him during the day's march. They "supposed him to have been in the company," says Luke; and it was only after seeking for him "among their kinsfolk and their acquaintance," that they discovered he had been left behind. They returned to Jerusalem, and found him in the temple, sitting in the midst of the doctors, both hearing them and asking them questions. And all that heard him were astonished at his understanding and his answers. So absorbed was he in this employment, as if it were his proper concern, that, when his mother complained of the uneasiness they had suffered on his account, he expressed surprise that they should have spent any time in searching for him; they should have come directly to the temple; for they might know that he would be engaged in his Father's business. Yet at their command he immediately left the place, and went with them to Galilee, and there remained subject to them as a dutiful son.

We are often reminded that Jesus set an example for our imitation. This is true of his childhood as well as of his age. He seems to have been conscious of his greatness, yet he did not presume upon it. He was docile and humble, reverent and obedient to his parents. It would be well if many young persons, who treat their parents with disrespect, and show that they feel themselves superior to their authority, would copy the meekness and submission which Jesus exhibited. They might learn from him how becoming in the young is respect to their elders, and that true greatness is not inconsistent with humility. How many there are who feel above the business which their fathers follow, and would think themselves demeaned by engaging in it! Yet Jesus wrought in the workshop with Joseph and his sons, made himself of no reputation, took the form of a servant, and thought it not at all inconsistent with the honors to which he was appointed.

How interesting to think of him during those years of his childhood and youth! What must have been his thoughts and emotions, the visions that occupied his young mind, the contemplations and anticipations that filled and agitated his bosom, as he quietly moved on like other men, and yet knew himself to be so different from them; among them, but not of them; not understood by them, nor enjoying any sympathy with them on the great subject that occupied his whole soul. Even his brethren did not feel with him, nor perceive in him anything uncommon. They did not believe in him. Perhaps with his mother he communed of all that was within him; but excepting her, who was there to share or comprehend his feelings, except his Father in heaven? With him his communion must have been near and precious; and he undoubtedly felt then, what he afterwards expressed, "I am not alone, for the Father is with me."

But we cannot hope to enter fully into this portion of our Lord's life, because no trustworthy history of it remains to us. The evangelists tell us nothing concerning it; and the book called *The Infancy of Jesus*, which pretends to instruct on this subject, is without authority, and altogether undeserving of credit. It was written by some superstitious person of an early age, who thought to gratify the natural curiosity of Christians respecting their Master, by recording wonderful stories of his childhood. But nothing can be more puerile and worthless than most of them are. It is amazing that they could have been for a moment credited. The person who invented or recorded them had no true understanding of what constitutes the glory and beauty of our Lord's character, and did not perceive how totally inconsistent with it are the foolish tales he recited. They are wanton and useless; they have nothing of dignity or divinity in them. When we turn from them to the narratives of the Scripture history, we find ourselves in a different world; we feel that all is divine and worthy the Son of God; we are sure that no man could have done his works except God were with him, and no man could have imagined them except they were really done. Amongst all the books in the world we can find no such striking instance of the difference between truth and falsehood as we find here. And Providence seems to have permitted those miserable fables to descend to our time, for the purpose of showing us this difference, and convincing us more satisfactorily of the absolute divinity and truth of the real Gospels.

CHAPTER III.

STATE OF JUDÆA. — EXPECTATION OF THE MESSIAH. — SIGNS OF HIS COMING. — HIS FORERUNNER.

In order to understand aright the circumstances and spirit of our Saviour's ministry, it is necessary to know many things respecting the state of the country and the history of the times in which he lived. There was much in them that was peculiar, and the knowledge of which will aid us to interpret our Lord's character, works, and manner of teaching, as well as his reception and success.

I have already said that the Jewish nation was in a state of degeneracy and decay. It was now just about a thousand years since it was at its height of prosperity, in the glorious reign of Solomon. The period of its greatness had been brief, for it was abused. Corruption of morals and of religion came in with prosperity. Immediately upon Solomon's death, ten of the tribes revolted, and set up a separate government under a separate king. From that day we read of two kingdoms, — that of Judah, comprehending only the two tribes of Judah and Benjamin, whose capital was Jerusalem; and that of Israel, which comprised the other ten tribes, and whose capital was Samaria. These two nations continued to exist by the side of each other, sometimes at war, sometimes at peace, for two hundred and fifty-four years. The kingdom of the ten tribes was then conquered by Shalmanezer, king of Assyria, and the people were carried into captivity. Here their history ends. What became of them never has been discovered. Some suppose that they were utterly destroyed, some that they were scattered over the various countries of Assyria, and many have fancied that their descendants still exist in Asia, Africa, or America. But this is all uncertain. It is more important to observe that their country was not wholly depopulated; some of the people were left in the land; and Shalmanezer planted among them colonies of idolaters, who mixed with them, and formed a new nation. This was the nation of the Samaritans, of which we read in the New Testament, — a nation hateful to the Jews, because it was descended in part from heathen ancestors, and yet professed to hold the law of Moses in a purer form than the Jews. Such was the fate of the kingdom of Israel.

The kingdom of Judah continued to flourish for one hundred and thirty-four years after the captivity of Israel. It was then overthrown by Nebuchadnezzar, king of Babylon, and the people were carried into captivity for seventy years. At the end of this period they were restored to their country; but they never recovered their former greatness. They were sometimes tributary to other nations, and sometimes governed by their own rulers; sometimes favored and sometimes oppressed by the powerful princes around them. On the whole, their condition was far from prosperous. Even the voice of prophecy ceased to be heard, and God withdrew the signs of his special interposition. No prophet appeared among them after they had been one hundred years returned from Babylon. They seemed to be given up to darkness, both political and religious. The family of the Maccabees at one period arose, and by its patriotism and talents cast a temporary brightness on the condition of the country. But this soon passed away. The people were too corrupt and too weak to maintain their rights against other nations, or to remain united among themselves. They divided into parties under two brothers, Aristobulus and Hyrcanus, who contended for the power. The quarrel was decided by an appeal to Pompey, the Roman general, who espoused the party of Hyrcanus, marched his legions to Jerusalem, besieged and took it, and subjected the whole country to the Roman government. This was sixty-three years before the birth of our Saviour.

But though the independence of the country was gone, the people were still allowed the exercise of their former customs and of their peculiar religious institutions and laws. The government was for a long time unsettled, until Herod, surnamed the Great, was made king by the Romans about thirty years before Christ. He was a courageous and cunning man ; a brave soldier, a good general, a lover of magnificence and pomp, but ambitious, deceitful, and cruel. He did much for the prosperity of the nation, ornamented Jerusalem in various ways, and rebuilt the temple at great expense and with great splendor. But his jealousy and cruelty caused him to be detested by the people. He put to death his own wife and children, and many other members of his family. No one could feel safe from his capricious cruelty. When about to die, he assembled the chief men of the nation at Jericho, and shut them up in the circus. Then he gave orders, that, at the moment of his death, the soldiers should be let in upon them, and put them all to the sword. For, he said, he knew that the Jews would rejoice at his death, and he was resolved to make them mourn. Happily these horrible orders were not executed, and there was probably unmixed joy at the tyrant's death. After knowing this, which is related by Josephus, the Jewish historian, we cannot think it incredible that he should put to death the infants of Bethlehem, for fear the new-born Saviour should escape. We understand, too, why all Jerusalem was troubled when the Magi inquired for the young king. They knew well enough that it would exasperate the jealous Herod, and lead to some deed of cruelty and blood. It has even been thought by some that he pretended to be himself the Messiah, and therefore would allow no one else to be so. Their reason for this is, that we read in the Evangelist of a sect of the Herodians, who are supposed to have favored his claims, and been his followers. If it were so, it might help to account yet more perfectly for his desire to slay the infant Christ. But it is altogether uncertain.

At the death of Herod, he divided his dominions between his three sons, Archelaus, Antipas, and Philip.

Archelaus had Judæa, Samaria, and Idumea. He reigned less than ten years, and, having been guilty of great injustice, was then deposed, and banished to Gaul, where he died. At his death his dominions became a province of the Roman Empire, of which, during our Saviour's ministry, Pontius Pilate was governor.

Herod Antipas possessed Galilee and Peræa. He is the Herod spoken of in the Gospels during

Luke iii.

our Lord's ministry. It was he who put John the Baptist to death, and to whom Pilate sent Jesus, that he might be tried, because he was a Galilean.

Herod Philip was tetrarch of Ituræa and Trachonitis, which lie opposite Galilee, on the other side of the Jordan. He is barely mentioned in the New Testament. He was a mild and just prince, and into his dominions Jesus retreated when he desired to avoid the plots of Herod Antipas.

It appears, then, that the country in which Jesus exercised his ministry was divided into three governments, — Galilee and Peræa under Herod, Judæa and Samaria under Pilate, and Trachonitis and Ituræa under Philip. Herod was styled *tetrarch*, and sometimes, though not rightfully, *king*. Pilate was simply *governor*, or, to use the Roman title, Procurator. Herod was tyrannical and cunning, well deserving the name, which our Lord gave him, of the Fox. Pilate was weak, cruel, rash, and obstinate. Both of them were at last banished by the Emperor for misgovernment, and Pilate in consequence destroyed himself. Philip was a good and just prince, and died quietly after a reign of thirty-seven years.

Such was the government of the country. It was no longer in the hands of the Jews, but of foreigners. The sceptre had departed from Judah, and the lawgiver from between her feet. It was, therefore, time to look for the Messiah; for the prophet had said that these things should not be until Shiloh come; which the Jews understood to mean the Messiah. Accordingly at this time they were eagerly looking out for him. When they saw the Roman soldiers garrisoned in their towns, and the Roman tax-gatherers collecting their money, and felt every day the wretchedness of their enslaved and impoverished condition, their hearts burned with impatience. They longed to throw off the yoke, to drive out the oppressors, and be free. They had read in the Prophets, that God would send them a mighty deliverer, the son of David, who should come amongst them in power and glory, and set up a kingdom over the whole earth. He was known among them by the name of *the Messiah*, or *the Christ;* that is, *the Anointed.* They thought it time for him to appear, for the signs spoken of by Moses and Daniel seemed to be fulfilled. They were waiting for him with eagerness. They trusted that he would free them from their bondage. They did not think of him as a *religious* teacher, coming to establish a spiritual kingdom. No; they were satisfied with their religion, and proud of their goodness. They wanted nothing but to be rid of the Romans, and have their country restored to the power and greatness of the days of David and Solomon. This they expected to be done. They were ready to rise in arms, and fight for it. And it was because Jesus would not do this for them, that they pronounced him a deceiver, and put him to death.

We shall find, as we proceed, a great many proofs that this was the state of mind among the people, and shall have frequent occasion to refer to it.

It is remarkable, that this expectation of some extraordinary person being about to appear was not confined to the Jews, but existed in other nations. Perhaps they had learned it of the Jews, who were to be found in every part of the world, and who everywhere carried their Scriptures with them. Hence we see how it happened, that, when the star appeared in the East, the Magi at once knew its meaning. And when they came to Jerusalem, inquiring for the new-born king, Herod, though troubled, was not surprised at it; but simply asked, Where is the Christ to be born? He and the people were evidently expecting his birth. Simeon, too, was waiting for him in the temple.

In this state of mind the people continued, and undoubtedly grew more and more impatient, the longer his coming was delayed. Their oppression was more and more intolerable, and they were ready to seize upon every incident which gave the slightest prospect of relief. Thus, at the enrolment and taxation under Cyrenius, they flew to arms, and made resistance under many leaders; among whom was probably Theudas, mentioned by Gamaliel in the sixth chapter of Acts. A few years afterwards, another similar insurrection took place in Galilee, on occasion of a second taxation. We do not know that any of the leaders in either instance pretended to be the Messiah; but it is not improbable that they did so, as such pretensions were very common afterwards. What is to be remarked is the restless condition of the people, and their readiness to follow any leader who promised them relief.

At this moment there appeared in the midst of them, in the desert country of Judæa, and not thirty miles from Jerusalem, an austere man, clothed like a hermit, and denouncing sin like one of the ancient Prophets. The attention of the people was turned to him at once. Perhaps, said they, this is he whom we are expecting. There was much in his appearance to favor the idea. Refusing the delicacies of cultivated life, he lived frugally on locusts, which are freely used as food in that part of the world, and wild honey. He was coarsely clothed in a garment of camel's hair, with a leathern girdle about his loins. He preached boldly to the people, like another Elijah, and cried, "Repent, for the king-

Matthew iii. Mark i. Luke iii.

dom of heaven is at hand." He also did what was a new and striking thing, — he *baptized* those who followed him. It was an old custom to baptize heathen persons when they became converts to Judaism; but it was a new thing to baptize Jews. He declared it to be in preparation for the "kingdom of God," that is, the reign of the Messiah. The people therefore, as Luke says, "were in expectation, and all men mused in their hearts whether he were the Christ or not." They thronged to him from Jerusalem, and all Judæa, and were baptized of him in the Jordan, confessing their sins, and anxiously inquiring for the Messiah. Even the chief men of the nation were excited; and a formal deputation of priests and Levites was sent out to him from Jerusalem, while he was at Bethabara beyond Jordan, about thirty-five miles distant, to inquire of him whether he were the Christ, or whether they must wait yet longer for his appearance. John acknowledged to them that he was not; that he was only come to prepare the way for the Christ, agreeably to the prediction of Isaiah, "I am the voice of one crying in the wilderness, Prepare ye the way of the Lord, make his paths straight."

The people were therefore satisfied that he was not the Messiah; but they honored him as a great prophet, and he preached to them with boldness

John i.

and severity. When he saw Pharisees and Sadducees coming to his baptism, whom he knew to be hypocritical and worldly, he cried out to them: "O generation of vipers, who hath warned you to flee from the wrath to come? Bring forth fruit meet for repentance." He did not spare them, though they were members of the most powerful sects in the land. To the publicans also, and soldiers, who came to him, he gave appropriate warning and instruction. And, in a word, he did what he could to rouse the nation from its sinful condition, and prepare it to receive in a right spirit the great messenger who was to succeed him. He undoubtedly produced some effect; but the people were too corrupt to be easily reformed. Indeed, they were so intent on having a Messiah who should lead them to political freedom and glory, that they had little relish for moral exhortation and religious duty.

CHAPTER IV.

THE BAPTISM OF JESUS. — HIS TEMPTATION.

THE time at length arrived when Jesus should enter on his public work. He had reached the age of thirty years, the period prescribed in the law for the induction of the priests into their office. Hitherto he had lived in retirement, undistinguished from the men about him. He had been making no visible preparation for the great duties he was to perform. He attended no distinguished school; he was brought up at the feet of no learned Rabbi or eminent philosopher; it is not certain that he had learned, as men learn, the very elements of knowledge. Having, therefore, no human attainments to fit him for his arduous office, he must be qualified for it by supernatural endowments. Nothing but the consciousness of possessing these could embolden and enable the lowly Galilean to undertake the religious reformation of his country and of the world.

The time being arrived, he left Nazareth, and went to the place where John was preaching and

Matthew iii. 13. Mark i. 9. Luke iii. 21.

baptizing on the banks of the Jordan. He went, like the rest of the people, to be baptized. Now John and Jesus, being related to each other through their mothers, who were cousins, were probably well acquainted, though they did not dwell in the same place; but John did not know that Jesus was the Messiah. So well, however, did he know the purity of his character, that when he saw him coming to be baptized, he was unwilling to allow it. It is more fit, said he, that you should baptize me, and do you come to me? But Jesus answered, that it was a duty to observe all religious ordinances, and this one ought not to be neglected. He did not need it as a sign of his sinfulness and repentance; but he wished to conform to it, because it was appointed of God. "Thus it becomes us to fulfil all righteousness," he said. John was satisfied with this explanation, and baptized him. Then came the moment for announcing the Messiah to the world. The heavens opened, and the spirit descended in visible form like a dove, and alighted on him; and at the same moment a voice was heard from heaven, saying, "This is my beloved Son, in whom I am well pleased."

This was the first public attestation to the Messiahship of Jesus. The arrival of the long-expected prophet was thus proclaimed. John, the forerunner, who had been waiting for him, and the people who were impatient to see him, were made certain that this was he; and he himself was both assured that he was not under a delusion, in supposing himself the chosen one of God, and received that gift of the spirit, "without measure," which was to fit him for his great work.

Under the influence of this spirit he immediately went up from the Jordan, and retired into the heart of the desert. His mind was full of the thoughts which the greatness of the occasion excited. He went by himself, away from human society, to meditate on the wonders of his condition, to contemplate the labors before him, and to commune with God. From the humble village of Nazareth, from the obscurity of cottage life, he was to go forth as a prophet and preacher, to stand in the city of his people, and amongst the powerful and learned men of his time. He was to leave the labors of the artisan for the toils of a religious ministry, to bear the last messages of God to Judah, and to change the religion of the world. What a moment was this! What wonder that he felt inclined, that he felt it necessary, to seclude himself! He could have no thought for anything but the toils and trials before him, and for communion with his own soul and his Father.

He wandered into the desert. It does not follow, because a place is called *desert* in the Scriptures, that it is therefore wholly wild and savage. It may mean any uninhabited and uncultivated place, even though it were fruitful. The uninhabited places adjoining the towns were called *deserts*, yet they were frequently excellent pasturage. But the vast wilderness of Judæa, stretching along the Dead Sea to the south of Jerusalem, was, in some parts, extremely desolate. It was barren, rocky, and mountainous. And as Mark says that Jesus was with the "wild beasts," he probably retreated into the wildest of these places, where even fruits and berries could not be found sufficient to satisfy his hunger.

At length he felt the consequences of so long fasting. He was weary and weak. He was hungry, and craved food. And then it was, when thus worn with the fatigue of much watching and abstinence, that he was exposed to the temptations so fearfully described by the Evangelists. The history of those temptations has exercised the minds of learned men, who have explained them in many different ways. It is not necessary here to enter into the discussion of what is difficult. There is enough that is plain. We read, in the Epistle to the Hebrews, that Jesus was "tempted in all points like as we are, yet without sin." So it was in these temptations in the wilderness.

Matthew iv. Mark i. 12. Luke iv.

They came upon him when hungry and faint, and when it might seem a small thing to use his power of working miracles, in order to change stones into bread, and satisfy his exhausted nature. But he would not do it, for he felt that the Divine power had been imparted to him for no such selfish purposes. Neither would he yield to the temptation to make himself such a Messiah as the Jews were expecting, and seize upon the kingdoms and glory of the world. This he could easily have accomplished; but it would have been unfaithfulness to God and duty. Neither would he draw on himself the admiration and easy reception of the people, by descending into the midst of them, as if borne on angels' wings, from the pinnacle of the temple. He resisted every suggestion to gratify and aggrandize himself. Neither bodily suffering, nor the offers of worldly greatness, nor the desire of human applause, could divert him from what he knew to be his duty. In these things he was tempted as we are (and they are the temptations to which men most frequently yield), yet it was without sin. He came from them untouched; and he has thus taught us, that true greatness consists in resisting evil, and adhering steadfastly to duty.

There is much in this incident particularly suited to impress and instruct the young. They are just entering on the work of life, as Jesus was just entering on his ministry. They are beset with temptations which would turn them aside from duty. They are tempted by sensual and worldly gratifications, by appetite and passion, by wealth and pleasure, by honor and applause. They are tempted to sacrifice principle to policy, to abandon duty for interest, to forget their responsibility to God in their desire to secure the favor of man. Let them learn of Jesus. His example will teach them to encounter and resist. Let them do as he did, — promptly silence the tempter, refuse to hear the evil suggestion, and summon up to their aid the strong power of God's holy word. If they thus resist, they will overcome. The great conflict of virtue will be achieved in the beginning of their course, and their subsequent path will be comparatively plain and easy.

CHAPTER V.

GENERAL OUTLINE OF OUR LORD'S MINISTRY.—CALLING OF THE FIRST FIVE DISCIPLES AT BETHABARA.—THE FIRST MIRACLE.

It would greatly aid to the clear understanding of the course of our Saviour's life, if we were able to give dates to the several events. This, however, with regard to the greater part of them, is impossible. The Evangelists have marked very few of them in such a way that we can determine the precise time at which they took place. They do not even pretend to relate them all in the order in which they occurred. So far were they from thinking this a matter of great importance, that they have not so much as informed us how long the ministry of Christ lasted. Consequently there have been very various opinions on this point. Many persons suppose it to have continued about three years. Some think it could have been no longer than about a year. And others have fancied it to have been extended through many years.

It is not possible to examine here the reasons on which these several opinions are founded. I can only say, that, on the whole, I believe the second to be the most probable. It was the opinion entertained by the early Christians; and it is favored by the general course and character of the Gospel narratives. There were three great annual festivals in the Jewish Church, at which all the men were expected to appear at Jerusalem, and at which, therefore, we must suppose Jesus to have faithfully attended. The Evangelist John has recorded his visits to Jerusalem; and we find that he makes mention of a Passover, of a feast of Tabernacles, of a feast between them, which must have been that of the Pentecost, and of another Passover. This exactly makes out the festivals in their proper order, for a little more than one year. The other three Evangelists relate what took place in the country, and omit his visits to the city. We thus have, in John's Gospel, the regular account of what our Lord did in Jerusalem at four several festivals, and, in the other Evangelists, a relation of what he did at other times and places. The present history is arranged on this principle. The Passover mentioned in the sixth chapter of John being regarded as that at which our Lord suffered, the events of that chapter are transposed accordingly. The whole scheme thus becomes simple and probable, and is attended with fewer difficulties than perhaps any other.*

* This is the plan proposed by Dr. Carpenter, in his *Geogra-*

A brief preliminary survey of the order and connection of events will facilitate a clear apprehension of the history. It may be observed, then, that our Saviour's ministry naturally divides itself into five parts, corresponding to the several visits which he made to Jerusalem. His home was in Galilee; and thence he travelled to Jerusalem five times, on occasion of five several festivals, — the Passover, the feast of Pentecost, the feast of Tabernacles, the feast of Dedication, and the Passover a second time.

1. At what time of year his baptism took place, we have no means of ascertaining; perhaps in January. He then spent forty days in the desert, returned to Galilee, wrought his first miracle at Cana, and went up to attend the Passover at Jerusalem. In the year A. D. 29, this festival occurred on the 19th of March. This date is certain, for it depends on astronomical calculation.

phy of the New Testament, and illustrated in the *Harmony* recently published in Boston, under the care of Professor Palfrey (by Gray and Bowen). I have seen cause to vary from it very little. It commends itself by its simplicity and ingenuity. In explanation of the transposition of the sixth chapter of John, it is to be observed, that the feeding of the five thousand is there said to have taken place when "the Passover was nigh." According to the other Evangelists, it took place not long before the *last* Passover. It seems proper to give to the event the same date in the narrative which the latter have given to it; for they specify *which* Passover was nigh, which John does not.

2. From this Passover he abode in Galilee till he returned to attend the feast of Pentecost in Jerusalem, the 8th of May.

3. He spent the summer in Galilee, but we have no particulars respecting his employment. He returned to Jerusalem on the 16th of September, the third day of the feast of Tabernacles.

4. At the close of the feast he returned home to Galilee, and then began the most active portion of his ministry. He travelled twice over Galilee, and sent out the twelve apostles and the seventy disciples. He came to Jerusalem to the feast of Dedication on the 26th of November.

5. The next interval he spent partly in Galilee, partly on the other side of the Jordan, partly in journeying from place to place, and returned to Jerusalem at the Passover in April. On Friday, the 7th of April, he was crucified; and the ascension consequently took place on the 11th of May.

On looking attentively at this statement, it will be seen, that our Lord's ministry, from his baptism to his death, lasted about one year and three months; and that far the greater portion of the records of the Evangelists relate to the last eight months. Indeed, ten of the twenty-one chapters of John are occupied with the narrative of the last six days. It may be useful to bear in mind this proportion between the several parts of his ministry.

As we cannot determine the precise date of the baptism, we cannot tell on what day he returned from his retirement of forty days in the wilderness. It appears to have been on the day before his return that the chief men of Jerusalem sent to John the Baptist the messengers already mentioned, to inquire whether he were the Christ. John denied it, as we have seen; but assured them, at the same time, that the Messiah was standing amongst them, though they knew him not. He then expressed his sense of his own inferiority, by adding, that he was not worthy to unloose the shoes' latchet of that eminent person. The day after John's interview with the deputation from Jerusalem, Jesus, returning from his temptation, arrived at the place where John was; and John pointed to him as the person of whom he had spoken. "Behold the Lamb of God, that taketh away the sin of the world! This is he of whom I said, After me cometh a man who is preferred before me, for he was before me."

This declaration of course excited the attention of those who heard it. Many would not give it credit, for they had no idea that the Messiah could appear in a humble form. But others would think differently; and those who were most devoted to John as his disciples would be most likely to put trust in his assertion. When, therefore, he

John i.

again, the next day, pointed to Jesus as he passed by, it is not strange that two of them immediately followed him, and sought to introduce themselves to him. One of these was Andrew, and the other is mentioned in such a way by the Evangelist John, as to render it probable that it was himself. Jesus, perceiving their intention, turned to them, and kindly invited them to his lodgings. It was "about the tenth hour," — nearly evening; and they remained with him that day. We cannot help wishing that we had an account of this interview. How interesting it would be to know what passed between the young Messiah and the first two persons who joined themselves to him! The consequence was, that they were persuaded that this indeed was he; and Andrew, desirous that his brother Simon should partake of his own satisfaction, brought him at once and introduced him to Jesus. Jesus immediately gave proof of his wonderful knowledge of men, by saying to him, "Thou art Simon; thou shalt be called *Cephas*," or Peter, — that is, *a rock;* for he knew the energy of his character, and that his labors would be the foundation of the Church.

These three persons, all of the same place, Bethsaida, a small town near the lake of Galilee, were the first to whom was given the honor of joining themselves to the new prophet. They, as well as he, were at a distance from their homes.

They had come to Bethabara, a distance of at least seventy miles, on account of the baptism of John. By his preaching, their minds had been in some measure prepared to embrace the Saviour, and they readily became his disciples. There were others there also, from the same part of the country. Philip, a townsman of Andrew and Peter, was invited to join them. No sooner had he done this, than he sought to draw a friend of his, Nathanael, into the company. Whether he too was a townsman, we do not know; but he was a sincere man, who, with all his goodness of heart, had much of the common prejudice against Nazareth. And when he heard that the person whom his friend was so anxious to have him see was from that despised village, he asked, with a sneer, "Can any good thing come out of Nazareth?" Philip, instead of reasoning with him, simply replied, "Come and see"; — the most sensible answer he could have given, and the best answer to be given to all who pretend to doubt whether anything good can come from Christ's religion. Jesus knew the character and heart of Nathanael, and, as soon as he saw him, uttered the memorable eulogium, "Behold an Israelite indeed, in whom is no guile." When Nathanael expressed surprise at finding himself known, Jesus astonished him by still another proof of unexpected knowledge. By this he was convinced, and exclaimed,

"Rabbi, thou art the Son of God, thou art the King of Israel." In this reply we have the earliest profession of faith in Christ which is recorded in the Gospels. Jesus received it graciously, and assured Nathanael, in reply, that he should see greater things yet; that he should witness the most incontestable supernatural proofs of his intercourse with heaven; — "Ye shall see the heavens open, and the angels of God ascending and descending on the Son of man." Here we observe that our Lord, at the very beginning of his ministry, used that striking figurative language for which he was always remarkable. It had an emphasis and grandeur suited to the greatness of him who spake it; it drew attention, and dwelt in the memory of those who heard it; and, though sometimes hard to be understood, was yet accommodated to the habits of the people whom he addressed, and was venerable in their eyes from its resemblance to the manner of their prophets.

Thus speedily did the Messiah collect the first adherents to his cause, — Andrew, John, Simon Peter, Philip, and Nathanael, — five honored and immortal names. They united themselves to the fortunes of Jesus of Nazareth, notwithstanding their prejudices against his town, and the humbleness of his appearance, because they had seen him, conversed with him, and judged for themselves of his pretensions.

And now, accompanied by this little band of friends, certainly by Philip, most probably by all, he left the banks of the Jordan, and turned his face homeward. We are left to imagine the meeting between him and his mother, when she saw the son of her hopes returned from his baptism, wearing at length the character she had so long waited for him to assume, and accompanied by followers who were pledged to him as their Lord.

Three days after his return, there was a marriage at the neighboring village of Cana, three miles distant, at which Jesus was present with his mother and disciples. Here Mary was desirous that he should make proof of his miraculous power, which as yet he had never done,—a power which she, with a feeling very natural in a mother, was impatient to have exhibited. A Jewish marriage was an occasion of great publicity and pomp. It lasted seven days. Mary seems to have had a peculiar interest in the present occasion, not improbably was occupied in superintending the celebration. She perceived that the supply of wine was insufficient. It seemed to her to offer a fit occasion for the exercise of her son's miraculous power. She suggested it to him. His reply intimates that this was a matter in which he could not allow her to interfere or ad-

John ii.

vise; that he should do miracles when the proper time came, but that no one must presume to control him. Yet, as he perceived it to be a case of real embarrassment to the parties, who were probably poor, and he was always ready, in his overflowing good-will, to do any kindness which was not inconsistent with his religious duty, he did what his mother had suggested, and signalized the festival by the first of those miracles whose power has converted the world. With beautiful simplicity the Evangelist relates all the particulars as they took place, and how the master of the ceremonies praised the wine as better than any that had been drunk before. Thus, he adds, did Jesus manifest his glory, and his disciples believed on him; they were certain now, since they were witnesses of the Divine power he possessed, that he was indeed the long-expected prophet.

From Cana he went down, with his mother, brothers, and disciples, to Capernaum, a village about eighteen miles distant on the western border of the lake. He remained there but a few days. The Passover was near at hand, and they were preparing to go, probably all in company, to join in its celebration at Jerusalem.

CHAPTER VI.

THE FIRST PASSOVER. — THE VISIT OF NICODEMUS. — THE RETURN THROUGH SAMARIA TO GALILEE. — THE WOMAN AT JACOB'S WELL.

THE Passover was the principal festival of the Jewish nation. It was appointed to commemorate the deliverance of the people from their bondage in Egypt, and received its name from the circumstance that the destroying angel, who was sent to slay the first-born of the Egyptians, *passed over* the houses of the Israelites. It was also called the Feast of Unleavened Bread, because no leavened bread might be eaten during its continuance. It lasted for seven days, and was observed with many appropriate ceremonies and sacrifices. The most remarkable was the sacrificing and eating of the paschal lamb, which took place on the first night. Each family slew its lamb, which was roasted whole, and eaten with many significant forms. The next day was signalized by the solemn offering in the temple of the first fruits of the barley-harvest. Sacrifices peculiar to the festival were offered every day, and the first and the last were especially holy.

This festival occurred in the spring, at the full moon of the vernal equinox. It was a festival for the whole people; and all the male inhabitants of the land were obliged to go up and keep it at the temple. At this time, therefore, Jesus, with his disciples and friends, left Capernaum for Jerusalem. It was a journey of about ninety miles, undoubtedly performed on foot; but evidently it could not be lonely, for the roads must have been thronged with the inhabitants pouring forth on the same errand. No incidents which took place on the journey are recorded. Our Lord was as yet little known; he travelled humbly and without observation. There were a few who knew what he was, but to most persons he appeared in no way distinguished from the other young men of his company.

Immediately on his arrival at the holy city he went up to the temple, that splendid structure, which was the delight and boast of every Jewish heart. It had been recently rebuilt with great magnificence by King Herod the Great; and was now glorious in all the freshness of its spacious porticos and marble pillars and costly ornaments. It stood on the summit of a lofty hill, overlooking the city, so that it was said, "Let us GO UP to the house of the Lord." The house itself was not larger than many of the ordinary churches of mod-

John ii. 13.

ern times. But it was surrounded by extensive courts, which were also called the temple, and are frequently meant when the temple is spoken of in the New Testament. These courts were one within the other, each surrounded by a wall, and paved with marble. The outer enclosure was called *the court of the Gentiles*, because it was open to them, but they might proceed no farther. The next enclosure was called *the court of the Israelites*, because they might enter this, but could proceed no farther. It was divided into two apartments, the outer of which was *the court of the women*. The third enclosure was called *the court of the priests*. Into this the priests only and Levites might enter. In this court stood THE TEMPLE with the altar of burnt-offerings before it. Here the sacrifices were offered. The people brought their offerings no farther than the wall, of one cubit high, which separated this court from that of the Israelites. The temple was divided into two parts; in the outermost of which stood the altar of incense, the table of shewbread, and the golden candlestick. Into this only the priests could enter. The inner apartment of the temple, separated from the outer by a splendid veil, was called the Holy of holies. Here were the cherubim and the ark of the covenant. No person could enter this but the high priest, and he only once a year, on an occasion of special solemnity, called the day of atonement.

Thus the several enclosures and apartments of the temple grew more and more holy as you proceeded. The outermost court was open to all persons, while the innermost apartment was open only to the highest religious minister on one solemn day. It is the outer court which is meant, when we read of the conversations that took place in the temple, and of children crying Hosanna there. It was evidently a place of ordinary resort, where the people daily congregated for conversation and business, and where multitudes must have been daily passing and repassing at the times of the sacrifices and the hours of prayer. How commodious it must have been for all such purposes of concourse may be perceived by remembering that it was a space of more than fourteen acres in extent. It was of a square form, each side a furlong in length, with a magnificent covered portico, or piazza, all around, like the cloisters of a monastery, supported by a hundred and sixty-two marble pillars of great size. No wonder that such a place was constantly frequented, and that it became a resort for purposes of business as well as religion. The offerings and sacrifices of the temple demanded a continual supply of cattle, lambs, and doves; and it was very convenient for the worshippers to find them ready at hand. Those who had these animals for sale were hence accustomed to sit with them in this court, and offer them for sale to the people as they passed in to the sacrifice; and for the accommodation of this traffic, money-changers set up their tables by their side.

Such was the scene which met the view of Jesus on his arrival at the sacred place. The people were so accustomed to the sight, that they did not perceive anything wrong in it. But he felt the profanation; and, as if the spirit of the old prophets had risen up within him, he took a whip of small cords, and drove the sheep and the oxen out of the court, and commanded the sellers of doves to take them away, and overset the tables of the money-changers. This bold act of religious zeal created, of course, no little excitement. His disciples, who were longing to see him take the character which belonged to him, were gratified at this spirited assumption of authority, and they applied to him the words used of the Psalmist, "The zeal of thy house hath consumed me." The people were amazed at an act which implied such consciousness of right and authority, and thought it possible that he might be the expected prophet. They accordingly came to him, and asked him to show them some sign in proof of his authority. As he knew what was in man and did not choose to commit himself to them, he answered them in a figurative expression, which could be perfectly understood only after his resurrection.

He pointed to that great event as the proof that he was from God. "Destroy this temple," said he, meaning the temple of his body, "and in three days I will raise it again." At that time his words were not understood; but after his crucifixion they were remembered, and served to confirm the truth of his pretensions to divine knowledge.

While he remained at Jerusalem, he wrought many miracles, which drew attention to him, and augmented the number of those who believed in him. He did not however disclose himself to them, for he knew that the time had not yet arrived when he could advantageously do so. He knew the nature of their expectations from him; therefore he would not trust them, nor commit himself to them.

The most remarkable circumstance which occurred during this period was the visit which he received from one of the rulers, whose name was Nicodemus. This man, a person of some consequence in the nation, had become strongly interested in what he had seen and heard of the wonderful young stranger from Galilee, and desired to ascertain, by means of a personal interview, whether he were the Messiah or not. Accordingly he came to Jesus; but by night, when he would be least liable to be observed. For he

John iii.

chose to satisfy himself fully, before he would attract attention to his movements. He saluted our Lord respectfully, and assured him that he believed he came from God; for, said he, "no man can do these miracles which thou dost, except God were with him." He thus evidently expressed a readiness to join himself to the Saviour; but as our Lord knew that his views were not right, that he was looking for a worldly Messiah and hoping an earthly reward, he did not encourage his advances, but immediately began to show him his mistake, and explain the true nature of the kingdom of the Messiah. He taught him that it was not of this world, not temporal, but spiritual; that, in order to enter it, one must give up all his worldly views and temporal expectations, and fit himself, by spiritual-mindedness, for a spiritual kingdom. These great truths he clothed, according to his manner, in bold and strong, but natural figures. But it was not easy for the Jewish ruler to understand them. They were not consonant to his prejudices or his desires. And he went away without openly attaching himself to the cause of Jesus. Yet such an impression did the conversation make on his mind, that he appears ever to have regarded our Lord with reverence and attachment. We find him, some time afterward, one of the few who dared to speak in his defence and who honored him in his death.

We may trust that the memorable interview of that night produced its true effects on his soul; that the solemn words of Jesus taught him, as they have taught multitudes since, the superiority and necessity of a spiritual life, and roused him from his vain passions and worldly ambition to the sense of a higher existence.

The Passover being ended, Jesus and his disciples left Jerusalem, and took up their abode for a time somewhere near the river Jordan, in Judæa. Here he gained many followers, who were baptized into his faith; not however by his own hand, but by that of the disciples. John also was still baptizing, but had removed from Bethabara to Ænon, near Salim, in Samaria. This circumstance of two prophets being engaged in collecting and baptizing followers at the same time naturally excited some speculation among the people. Some of John's disciples fell into an argument respecting it with a Jew, and they referred the question to John himself for his decision. These disciples appear to have been jealous for their master's honor, and could not well bear that another should attract more followers than he. But John had nothing of this feeling, and he endeavored to remove it from the mind of his disciples. He reminded them that he had always asserted that he was not himself the Christ, but greatly inferior to him. He now repeated his assertions, and went on to declare to them, in the strongest terms, the necessity of believing in the Son of God. In this way John quieted the minds of his disciples.

But there were others who were not so easily satisfied, and who loudly expressed their displeasure. These were the Pharisees, the leading sect amongst the Jews, the sect which comprised probably the principal part of the learned and influential men. The Pharisees professed to be more strictly and zealously devoted to the law than any others, and by their severe external sanctity and punctilious attention to the forms of religion, they secured the veneration of the multitude. They were scrupulous observers of the Sabbath, they kept frequent fasts, were exact in all washings, ostentatious in paying tithes, in repeating prayers, and in giving alms, professed great abhorrence at sinners, and even carried the show of sanctity into the phylacteries and fringes of their garments. Thus their appearance corresponded with their name, which meant *separated*, or *set apart*, from other men in holiness and piety; and their haughty treatment of all whom they considered sinners was of a piece with their high pretensions.

Such was the popular and predominant sect. Of course they were jealous to maintain their influence, and unfriendly to all persons and parties who would either rival them in the estimation of the people, or expose their true character. It could not but happen, that they would look with ill-will on any one who should assume to be a religious teacher, and not consult them and forward their purposes. It is plain, that, with their principles and character, no one could be received by them as the Messiah, unless he corresponded to their expectations, and in fact were one of the Pharisees. When therefore they heard of the bold procedure of a young man from Galilee, who had gone about cleansing the temple, and teaching the people, and baptizing followers independently of them, they were naturally displeased. His tone of instruction, too, was very unlike theirs, and tended to bring them into discredit. His simplicity and purity were disagreeable to their artifice and hypocrisy. They felt themselves rebuked by his modest but severe virtue. They therefore felt ill-disposed toward him. They could not listen to the idea that he was the Messiah. Surely the Messiah would be sent to the chiefs of the church, and not spring up from the dregs of the people. "Search and look," said they, "for out of Galilee ariseth no prophet."

On hearing that this new teacher was successful in gaining adherents, and that he baptized even greater numbers than John had done, they did not conceal their displeasure. In what manner they expressed it, we are not told; but we read that when Jesus heard of this, he left the place where he was, for he knew that it was not his duty to provoke opposition unnecessarily; and in order to avoid every occasion of complaint for the present, he quitted Judæa altogether, and returned to his own country of Galilee.

On his way to Galilee he necessarily passed through Samaria, which lies between that province and Judæa. At least this was the nearest and most convenient route, though the Jews sometimes took a more circuitous course; as we shall find that our Lord did on another occasion, in order to avoid the enmity of the Samaritans. It was on this journey that occurred one of the most interesting incidents of his ministry. At about the distance of forty miles from Jerusalem, just before reaching the famous mountains of Ebal and Gerizim, is the well which Jacob dug. It is to be seen there even to the present day; for in that country wells of water are so precious, that they are kept with the greatest care generation after generation. At about midday, our Saviour reached this well, and sat down to rest himself, while his disciples went forward to Sychar to purchase provisions for their refreshment. This town lay at nearly a mile's distance. It is the same

John iv.

which is called Shechem in the Old Testament. It stands in a beautiful, romantic, and fertile spot between the mountains of Ebal and Gerizim, and is to this day one of the most flourishing towns in Palestine. It was for a long time the capital of Samaria.

While Jesus sat waiting at the well, a woman came from the city to draw water. He immediately entered into conversation with her. This is a circumstance which marks his character. A common Jew would not have done so. A scribe, a priest, or a pharisee would have esteemed himself dishonored by so doing. Not only was it considered improper to converse with a woman publicly, but the Jews and Samaritans were inveterate enemies. They had no intercourse with each other; and it shows something in Jesus greatly superior to the prejudices of the times and the people, that he so readily conversed, not only with a woman, but with a Samaritan.

The woman herself was astonished at his addressing her. "How is it that thou," she exclaimed, "being a Jew, dost ask drink of me, who am a Samaritan?" She must have been still more astonished at his reply, and the turn which he gave to the conversation. For our Lord, agreeably to his uniform custom of drawing religious instruction from every incident, immediately took occasion to speak of that living water, of which if a man drink, he shall never thirst again. He awakened her curiosity, he excited her desire to know more, he alluded to some private circumstances in her life, and she saw that he was no common person, but a prophet. She therefore seized the opportunity to ask his judgment respecting that great question which divided the Jews and Samaritans, namely, whether the temple at Jerusalem or the mount of Gerizim was the true place of worship. Jesus replied, that this was no longer a question of any consequence; that a new order of things was about to be introduced; that all merely local worship and all limited service was to cease. "Woman, believe me, the hour cometh, when ye shall neither in this mountain, nor yet at Jerusalem, worship the Father. But the hour cometh, and now is, when the true worshippers shall worship the Father in spirit and in truth: for the Father seeketh such to worship him. God is a spirit: and they that worship him must worship him in spirit and in truth."

This doctrine was as new to the woman as it was grand and glorious. But she did not appear fully to enter into the meaning of it; it was too great for her to take in at once; and she answered our Lord by observing, that, when the Messiah should come, they undoubtedly should be fully instructed in this matter. Jesus at once, in the simplest manner, discovered himself to her. "I that speak unto thee am he." The woman, struck with astonishment, answered not a word, but put down her water-pot, and went back to the city to tell what she had seen and heard. "Come, see a man who told me all things that ever I did; is not this the Messiah?" The people were easily excited by such a report, and returned with her to see the wonderful stranger.

Meantime the disciples came back to their Master, whom they had left hungry and weary; but he was too much engaged in the feelings and hopes to which this incident had given rise, to care for the food which they brought. His mind was full of the excitement of a benevolent hope, that here he had done some good, here he might make some converts. He pointed to the crowd of people coming from the city, and bade his followers observe how the fields were already ripe for the harvest, that they only needed to go forth and reap, and they should gather fruit unto life eternal. And when the Samaritans entreated him to abide with them, he gladly accepted the invitation, and remained there two days. The consequence was, that many believed on him. They heard him speak, and were convinced, as their country-woman had been at the well. And they said to her, "Now we believe, not because of thy saying, for we have heard him ourselves, and know that this is indeed the Christ, the Saviour of the world."

Having spent two days at Sychar, he proceeded on his journey into Galilee. Here he was received by the people with great respect, for they had known the things which he did in Jerusalem at the feast. Of the events which occurred during his visit, nothing is related, excepting the cure of a nobleman's son at Capernaum, which was the second miracle performed in Galilee. It was while our Lord was at Cana, that this nobleman, as he is called, (that is, probably, some officer in the employment of the government,) came from Capernaum, a distance of nearly twenty miles, entreating Jesus to heal his son. This seems to show confidence in his power to work miracles; but it appears from our Lord's reply, that it was mingled with a good deal of doubt and distrust; for, said he, "Except ye see signs and wonders, ye will not believe." But when the anxious father urgently repeated his request, and thus evinced a strong faith, Jesus granted more than he asked. He assured him of the immediate safety of his son, without departing from the spot. "Go thy way," said he; "thy son liveth." And the father found it so on his return.

Our Lord's residence in Galilee at this time must have been short; for on the occurrence of the feast of Pentecost, fifty days after that of the Passover, he again went up to Jerusalem.

CHAPTER VII.

THE FEAST OF PENTECOST. — THE SUMMER SPENT IN GALILEE. — THE FEAST OF TABERNACLES. — CONVERSATION WITH THE JEWS AT JERUSALEM.

THE Pentecost was a festival in commemoration of the giving of the law from Mount Sinai. This event took place fifty days after the departure of the Israelites from Egypt; consequently the Pentecost occurred fifty days after the Passover, and because it thus took place at the interval of seven weeks, it was called *the feast of weeks.* It was celebrated by the offering of the first fruits of the wheat-harvest, which at that time was gathered in, and by various additional sacrifices at the temple. It was one of the three great occasions on which all the males of the land were required to present themselves in religious solemnity before the Lord. Our Saviour, therefore, whose rule it was "to fulfil all righteousness," again went up to Jerusalem.

This visit to the city was signalized by the cure of an "impotent man," as he is styled in our

John v.

translation ; — one who had been disabled by disease for thirty-eight years. Jesus found him lying with a multitude of blind, lame, and crippled persons near a pool called Bethesda, whose waters at certain seasons were thought to possess a miraculous power of healing. As he had no friend to lift him into the water, Jesus took pity on him and healed him by his word.

This happened on the Sabbath day. When the strict and superstitious Jews saw the poor man walking away with his couch on his shoulders, they cried out against him for breaking the Sabbath. He defended himself by answering, that the person who healed him had said to him, "Take up thy bed and walk." Their displeasure was thus turned against Jesus, and they persecuted him for this profanation of the holy day. This gave rise to one of those striking conversations recorded by John, in which our Lord vindicated himself against the charge of irreligion and blasphemy, asserted his authority and dignity as the Son of God, warned his countrymen against the rejection of his claims, and reminded them of three proofs which they possessed that he came from God; — namely, the testimony of John the Baptist, the miraculous works he performed, and the voice from heaven which was heard at his baptism. It was in this discourse that occurred that solemn and sublime passage respecting a future state of retribution, of which Paley has said: * "Had Jesus Christ delivered no other declaration, he had pronounced a message of inestimable importance, and well worthy of that splendid apparatus of prophecy and miracles with which his mission was introduced and attested." This declaration was: "The hour is coming, in which all that are in the graves shall hear his voice, and shall come forth; they that have done good unto the resurrection of life, and they that have done evil unto the resurrection of condemnation."

But it was in vain that he addressed his holy doctrine and earnest warnings to the prejudiced minds of his countrymen. They would not hear him. They persecuted and sought to kill him. And therefore, says the Evangelist, he did not continue in Judæa, but retired again to Galilee.

It was now the opening of the summer. The feast of Pentecost occurred in May, and we hear nothing more of him until the feast of Tabernacles in September. As the summer in that climate is intensely hot and enervating, and consequently unfavorable to exertion, it seems probable that he spent it in comparative retirement. No record of any of his acts during this time has come down to us. We are left to fancy him passing his time in holy contemplation and devotion, occupied in

* Moral Philosophy, Book v. ch. ix. John vii. 1.

teaching and blessing the circle with which he was immediately connected, and preparing himself for the severe trials and toils of the more active months which were to follow.

The feast of Tabernacles, the third of the three great solemnities at which the men were obliged to go up to the temple, was instituted in commemoration of the sojourn of the Israelites in the wilderness, where for so many years they dwelt in tents or tabernacles. It occurred in the beginning of autumn, and lasted seven days, or, as some think, eight; the first and last being the most solemn. The manner of its celebration was peculiar. During its whole continuance, the people resided in tents, or arbors, constructed of the boughs of trees, and placed in the streets, in the outer court of the temple, and on the tops of the houses. On the first day, they gathered branches of the finest trees, willow and palm trees especially, and went with them in procession to the temple, and encompassed the altar of burnt-offerings, singing certain songs, and crying, "Hosanna!" Hence these branches were called *Hosanna;* and the last day was called the *Great Hosanna*, because on that day this ceremony was performed seven times. They also brought as offerings to the temple the first fruits of their second harvest, and consecrated the occasion by a great variety of sacrifices, as well as by dancing, music, and illuminations. In fact, this feast may be considered as the great Thanksgiving of the Jewish people. It was kept by joyous religious feasting, like the autumnal festival of New England, and, like that, occurred just when the fruits of the earth had been gathered in.

On the approach of this feast, when all men were preparing to go to Jerusalem, the brothers of Jesus urged him to accompany them. They had no belief in his Messiahship, and they pretended to accuse him of hiding himself from observation, because he had passed the summer quietly in Galilee. "For," said they, "no man doeth anything in secret, and yet seeketh himself to be known openly. If thou do these things, show thyself to the world." But he replied to them, that his time was not yet come; they could go at any time; he was not yet ready. They accordingly departed without him; and he afterwards followed them, privately, and apparently alone. He knew the jealousies and enmities which had already been excited, and he thought it prudent to avoid the occasions of offence which might arise from his travelling through the land when the ways were thronged with people. We shall have occasion to notice many remarkable instances of this reserve.

When the people were collected at the feast,

John vii.

there was immediately great inquiry made for him. They longed again to see the remarkable person, who, at the two preceding festivals, had done such wonderful works, and spoken such extraordinary doctrine, and who perhaps might prove to be the Messiah. "Where is he?" said they. His character and claims became the subject of eager discussion. Some took his part, and vindicated him. "He is a good man," they said, and by all means to be trusted. Others opposed him, and contended that he was deceiving the people. On the whole, the public sentiment was divided; but all these opinions were expressed in private conversation, for it had been decreed that all who acknowledged his Messiahship should suffer excommunication, and nothing came to an open result, "through fear of the Jews," says the Evangelist.

In the midst of all this, when the festival was about half over, Jesus arrived, and went directly up to the temple. In its sacred and crowded courts, he felt himself safe, and spoke freely as he had done before. What a sensation must his arrival have occasioned! How eagerly must the curious crowds have thronged about him! Some anxious to drink in the words of his divine wisdom; some solicitous to entrap him; all burning with vehement feeling, because they hoped, or feared, that he might prove their long-desired prophet.

Nothing seems to have surprised them more than the dignity and wisdom of his discourse. They knew where he had been bred, and what his education had been; and they could not guess how he should be so superior to other men. "How knoweth this man letters," said they, "having never learned?" Jesus gave them the only reply which could be given, the only explanation which was or could be satisfactory, — "My doctrine is not mine, but His that sent me." He then went on to expostulate with them on their injustice and wickedness toward him at his last visit; defended the act which had displeased them as a breach of the Sabbath; and ended with the exhortation, "Judge not according to appearance, but judge righteous judgment."

It is evident from the account of the Evangelist, that our Lord's address created a strong sensation among the people. They began to debate whether this were not the Messiah. Many believed on him; for, said they, very justly, can we suppose that the Messiah, when he comes, could do more miracles than this man has done? But others doubted and denied, and said this could not be he, because they knew whence he came, and no one was to know whence the Christ should come. For it seems to have been a common notion among the Jews of that period that the origin of the Messiah would be unknown.

This agitation among the people made the leaders and the Pharisees uneasy, and they thought it best to put an end to it by seizing Jesus. It appears to have continued day after day, and they could not tell what it might lead to. Therefore they sent officers to apprehend him. But the result was very different from what they had anticipated.

The last day of the feast was a great day. It was kept with extraordinary pomp and solemnity. Besides the additional processions, already mentioned, another was formed of yet greater significance. The people went out of the gate of the city to the fountain of Siloam, and, drawing its waters, bore them to the temple. Part of this water they there drank with loud acclamations, and, mingling the rest of it with wine, poured it out at the foot of the altar of burnt-offerings; singing meanwhile in loud chorus those words of Isaiah, "With joy shall ye draw water from the wells of salvation." The ceremony was in the highest degree animating and impressive. At the present time it must have been more than ever striking. For it was broken in upon by the voice of Jesus, who stood and cried, "If any man thirst, let him come to me and drink. He that believeth on me, as the Scripture hath said, there shall flow from him rivers of living water"; — he shall be filled with the spirit of holiness and truth, and from him, like a fountain of pure waters, it shall flow forth upon all around him. The consequence of this address was a new movement among the people. Many were confirmed in the belief that this was the Messiah. "Of a truth," they cried, "this is the Prophet; this is the Christ." But others insisted that the Christ could not be a Galilean; and thus opinions were still divided.

In the mean time, the officers who had been sent to seize him were overcome with admiration at what they saw and heard, and returned to their employers without even making the attempt to take him. "Why have ye not brought him?" asked the Pharisees. The officers could only reply, "Never man spake like this man." The reply contains volumes. But it only irritated the Pharisees, who gave vent to their feelings in violent language. "Are ye also deceived?" said they. "Have any of the rulers or of the Pharisees believed on him? But this people, this rabble, that knoweth not the law, is accursed." Here Nicodemus ventured gently to interfere, and remind them that no man was to be condemned without a trial. But he only drew the storm upon himself. What, said they, "art thou also of Galilee? Search and look; for out of Galilee ariseth no prophet." Here the matter ended, and the council broke up. Jesus retired from the city, and passed the night on the Mount of Olives.

In the morning he returned to the temple. The people again collected around him, and he sat down beneath the portico, and taught. While he was thus engaged, the scribes and Pharisees, who had been defeated in their attack upon him the day before, planned a new assault, and instead of an open attack attempted to surprise him by artifice. They brought to him a woman who had been detected in a crime; and, addressing him in very respectful language, asked him his opinion whether she ought to be stoned agreeably to the law of Moses. This they did, says the Evangelist, " tempting him, that they might have whereof to accuse him." For if he should say, Yes, then they hoped the people would do according to his word and stone her; in which case he could be brought before the Roman power as inciting to tumult and sedition; for the Romans did not allow the Jews the right to put any one to death. And on the other hand, if he should say, No, they could exhibit him to the people as one who set aside the law of Moses, and who therefore deserved no respect. Thus they thought themselves sure of entangling him. But his divine sagacity enabled him to escape the snare. Instead of a direct answer, he stooped down, and wrote

John viii.

upon the pavement with his finger, as if he either did not hear them, or was engaged in considering what they had said. When they urged him for a reply, he lifted up his head, and said, " He that is without sin among you, let him first cast a stone at her." He then returned to his employment. The accusers were confounded. They felt conscience-stricken. And, having nothing to say, they stole away one after another, and left the woman alone. When our Lord perceived this, his gentleness and compassion were displayed in his treatment of the woman as remarkably as his skill had been in baffling her accusers. He would not assume the authority of the law to condemn her, and dismissed her with an admonition to sin no more. " Hath no man condemned thee ? " he asked. — " No man, Lord." — " Neither do I condemn thee. Go, and sin no more."

He then continued his conversation in the temple with the Pharisees and other Jews ; replying to their questions, vindicating his character, expostulating with them because of their sins, and asserting his own high dignity and authority. Some believed on him ; many cavilled ; and finally, on their threatening to stone him, he hid himself and went out of the temple, and escaped from their hands.

It is not perfectly clear whether the incident next recorded by the Evangelist occurred on the same day with what we have just related. It probably did. As he passed through the streets of the city after leaving the temple, he fell in with a man blind from his birth; and, nothing deterred by the dangers he had just escaped, he exerted his miraculous power to give him sight. This was a miracle particularly adapted to excite attention, because none similar had ever been wrought. It was without example in the whole history of the nation. From this circumstance, as well as from its taking place just at this time, it immediately underwent a strict scrutiny. It was an open, wonderful, unexampled display of power. The enemies of Jesus saw that it was likely to produce a great effect. They therefore made it their object to discredit it, if possible.

They first tried to make it appear that no miracle had been wrought. But the neighbors of the man testified that he had been blind, and his parents confirmed the testimony. "We know," said they, "that this is our son, and that he was born blind; but by what means he now seeth, we know not, or who hath opened his eyes, we know not; he is of age, ask him." Thus there was no doubt of the *fact*, though the parents dared not say, as their son boldly did, that Jesus was a prophet.

The Pharisees next tried to prove that, notwithstanding this miracle, he was no prophet.

John ix.

He had broken the Sabbath. He was a sinner. They knew nothing about him; they knew that God spoke by Moses, but as for this man, they knew not whence he was. It was a bold and generous reply of the poor man who had been healed: "Why, herein is a marvellous thing, that ye know not whence he is, and yet he hath opened mine eyes. If this man were not of God, he could do nothing." At this the Pharisees were irritated; "Thou wast altogether born in sin, and dost thou teach us?" And then, finding that they could neither prove the falsehood of the miracle, nor persuade the people that it was not done by divine power, they cast him out of the synagogue; that is, they excommunicated him, — a severe punishment, and the highest in their power to inflict. They had already threatened it to all who should confess Jesus to be the Messiah, and it was the only answer they could make to the reasoning of this poor beggar.

But the blind man was not wholly forsaken. Jesus sought him in his trouble, and cheered him by a kind word, — nay, did him the honor of acknowledging to him, as he had yet done only to the Samaritan woman, that he was truly the Christ. So condescending and kind was our gracious Master; and so, to the present day, does his Gospel stoop to the forsaken and lowly, and whisper words of cheerful peace to their spirits.

From speaking to this humble and grateful individual, our Lord turned to address a word of admonition to the people who stood by. "For judgment I am come into this world," said he, "that they which see not might see, and that they which see might be made blind." This brought him once more into collision with the Pharisees, who ceased not to follow and persecute him. He still answered them as before, boldly yet prudently, and closed his address with the beautiful and affecting parable, in which he speaks of himself as the good shepherd, who lays down his life for the sheep. This parable, it is said, was not fully comprehended by those who heard it; but it has been full of a delightful meaning to believers in all ages since, and, like several of our Lord's discourses, was designed less for those around him than for those who should afterward believe in him. As regards the immediate effect, St. John says again, as he had said on other occasions, that there was a division among the hearers. Some cried out, "He has a demon and is mad; why do you listen to him?" Others insisted that his giving sight to the blind was a proof to the contrary, for demons could not cure blindness.

Here closes the account of those memorable scenes which took place at Jerusalem during his visit at the feast of Tabernacles. They are full of the deepest interest and instruction, and should be studied diligently in the chapters of John's Gospel, in which they are recorded at length. It is impossible, in a work like the present, to elucidate them more particularly. I have only been able to go into them so far as might disclose the exact posture of affairs, the state of the public mind respecting our Lord's character and claims, the increasing interest with which his teaching was attended, the industry and malice of his enemies, and the way which was thus opened for the greater activity of his ministry in time to come, as well as the sufferings and violence with which it closed.

It will be perceived that, thus far, the history has been drawn almost exclusively from the Gospel of John. We find nothing, since the baptism and temptation, recorded by the other Evangelists. The cause is plain. John was attached to our Saviour from the first; he probably accompanied him on his visits to Jerusalem at the several festivals, and was personally knowing to the scenes which he describes there. Matthew was called later; and he, therefore, as well as Luke and Mark, relates little till after the appointment of the twelve apostles, because until about that time he was not an eyewitness. We learn, also, why John relates little except what occurred at the festivals. During those periods he was in his Master's company; but in the intervals he returned to his employment on the lake of Galilee, and did not become a constant companion of Jesus until some time after the feast of Tabernacles. If it be asked why, in the subsequent narrative, he continued to confine himself to what occurred at the festivals, the answer is obvious. The other Evangelists, who wrote before he did, had related all else that was important, and it was apparently his plan to tell chiefly what they had omitted. Or perhaps, as they had given chiefly their Lord's ministry in the provinces, it was his plan to record his ministry in the city. The circumstances here mentioned are interesting in themselves, and they tend strongly to prove the probable correctness of the arrangement followed in the present work.

CHAPTER VIII.

IMPRISONMENT OF JOHN THE BAPTIST. — JESUS BEGINS HIS PUBLIC MINISTRY IN GALILEE. — SERMON ON THE MOUNT.

It was about this time that John the Baptist gave that offence to Herod, the tetrarch of Galilee, which occasioned his imprisonment, and finally led to his death. Herod had married Herodias, the wife of his brother Philip. John censured this as a sin; and Herodias, angry at his boldness and rebuke, instigated Herod to cast him into prison. Herod himself, we are told by Mark, had a great respect for John, and would willingly have spared him.

When Jesus heard of this, he left Jerusalem, and returned to Galilee. The ministry of his Forerunner was finished; and it was therefore time to commence his own in a more public and active form. Hitherto he had confined himself to a few places. His labor thus far seems to have been preliminary, a gradual preparation for that

Matthew xiv. 3, iv. 12. Mark vi. 17, i. 14.
Luke iv. 14, iii. 19.

zealous action which was to distinguish the later months of his life. Hitherto his forerunner, John had been occupied in preaching and preparing the way before him. But his mission was now ended; and therefore, as Mark declares, Jesus came into Galilee, preaching the gospel of the kingdom of God, and saying, "The time is fulfilled, and the kingdom of God is at hand. Repent ye, and believe the Gospel."

Thus he passed on preaching in the synagogues, till he reached Nazareth, his own town. Here too he went into the synagogue on the Sabbath day, according to his custom. It proved to be a memorable visit. He had been for some time absent, and the report of what had taken place during his visit at Jerusalem had undoubtedly reached the ears of his townsmen. They were naturally curious to see him on his return. They were very incredulous that this humble mechanic, whom they had known from his childhood as one of themselves, should turn out a prophet, and excite the wonder and attention of the whole people at the feast. They were eager to have the matter explained.

The synagogue was the Jewish place of worship, answering to our churches. The desk, or pulpit, from which the law was read and explained, stood in the centre of the building. The book of the law was kept in an ark, or chest, at one end (either the eastern end, or that which faced the temple), and was brought from it, at the time of worship, with great form. In front of this ark were placed the seats for the elders, called by our Saviour "the chief seats"; and facing them were the seats for the congregation. The women sat in a gallery apart, concealed from view by a lattice.

The service of the synagogue, like that of the Christian Church, consisted of prayers, the reading of the law, and the expounding it, or preaching. It was the custom to read through their sacred books once every year, a certain portion being allotted to every Sabbath. The Scriptures, like all ancient books, were written throughout on long strips of parchment, like long pieces of narrow cloth. These were rolled upon round pieces of wood, as ribbons are at the present day. When a person read the book, he unrolled it as he went on, and wound it up again on another roller. So that when he stopped reading, and laid down the book, it was partly on one roller and partly on another; and when he took it up again, and opened it, his eye fell at once on the place where he had left off. Whoever therefore was appointed to read the portion of the law on the Sabbath found the place, without difficulty, by merely opening the roll. There were no regularly appointed readers, but the rulers of the synagogue called upon any competent person to read the portion for the day.

When the rulers of the synagogue in Nazareth saw Jesus come in, they gave the book to him, and requested him to read. Jesus took the volume, and stood up. It opened, of course, at the stated place. It was that celebrated passage in Isaiah (chapter lxi.) in which the offices of the Messiah are described. We may imagine with what breathless silence he was listened to, as he read: "The spirit of the Lord is upon me, for he hath anointed me to preach the Gospel to the poor, he hath sent me to heal the brokenhearted, to proclaim deliverance to the captives and recovering of sight to the blind; to set at liberty them that were bruised; to preach the acceptable year of the Lord." And he closed the book, and gave it to the minister, that is, the attendant who brought it to him, and sat down. His sitting down was a signal that he intended to speak. And the eyes of all that were in the synagogue were fastened on him, — eager to know what he had to say respecting this prophecy. His first words were: "This day is this scripture fulfilled in your ears." And he went on to prove and illustrate this in such a manner, that he excited their admiration at the gracious words which he uttered, and they expressed their amazement at hearing such things from "Joseph's son." "Is not this the carpenter," said they, "the son of Mary, the brother of James and Joses and Juda and

Simon? and are not his sisters with us?" Therefore they were offended at him, says Mark. And when he went on to explain why he did not work miracles there, as well as in other places, telling them that their prejudices were such that it would be of no use,—that now, as well as in the days of Elijah, there was more hope of the Gentiles than of persons like them,—they became greatly exasperated. They rose up, Sabbath as it was, and thrust him from the city, intending to cast him down from the brow of the hill on which the city was built. But he passed through the midst of them, and departed in safety.

Having thus escaped the violence of the populace, he proceeded to Capernaum, and took up his abode there. This place became henceforth his principal residence. Its precise situation is not known; but it was on the western bank of the sea or lake of Galilee, not far from the northern corner. It appears to have been at this time the home of Andrew and Peter, who had formerly resided in the neighboring town of Bethsaida. These men had not yet permanently attached themselves to his company. They were still occupied at their own business, which was that of fishermen on the lake.

It was while thus engaged casting their nets into the water, that they were called away by Je-

Matthew iv. 13. Mark i. 16.

sus to be his attendants and ministers. They were already well known to him, being two of the five who had followed him from Bethabara to Galilee. And now that he had arrived at the important period of his ministry, when it was necessary that he should be attended by persons who might aid him, and be competent witnesses to the world of his life and teaching, these two were the first that he selected for that purpose. They readily left their business to devote themselves to him; and their partners, James and John, sons of Zebedee, did the same.

Thus provided with four permanent attendants, our Lord prepared for the more vigorous promulgation of his religion. He returned with them to Capernaum, and taught in the synagogue on the Sabbath. On that occasion, he for the first time performed the miracle of casting out an unclean spirit. This excited the strong amazement of the people, and helped greatly to extend his fame. On leaving the synagogue, he retired to the house of Peter, whose wife's mother lay ill of a fever, and he healed her by a word. The report of these two miracles being spread through the town, as soon as the day was ended, the people thronged to the house, bringing with them the sick of every disease; and he laid his hands on them and healed them.

Luke v. 1.

In this remarkable manner did he signalize this first Sabbath of his abode in Capernaum. It was the beginning of that conspicuous manifestation of himself by which the remainder of his life was marked. It formed an important era in his ministry. He seems to have regarded it as such. And therefore, rising early in the morning, he departed into a solitary place for the purpose of prayer to God. This was his custom when about to undertake an action of special importance; and he was now designing to follow up the work he had begun in Capernaum by an immediate visit to other places in Galilee. While thus engaged, his disciples sought him out, and entreated him to return to the town; for, said they, "all men seek thee"; so strong was the sensation produced by the deeds of the preceding day. He however declined to return, saying, "Let us go into the next towns, that I may preach there also; for therefore came I forth." Accordingly they proceeded on a circuit through the country, going from town to town, teaching in the synagogues, and working miracles. His fame rapidly spread as he went, and numbers constantly attended him. The crowd appears to have increased daily; and it was made up, not only of inhabitants of the towns through which he passed, but of persons who came from great distances, some from Jerusalem, and some from beyond the Jordan.

It is easy to understand the motives which brought them together. The appearance of a person so like the ancient prophets in his wisdom and miraculous gifts would at any time have attracted attention. But now there was something more; there was the hope of finding their promised deliverer. When they heard how Jesus spoke as possessing authority from heaven, and did the works of God, and proclaimed that the kingdom of God was nigh at hand, they hoped and believed that this was HE. As his miracles were multiplied, their hopes increased; and they crowded about him, that they might be ready for the disclosure of his designs, and seize at once the advantages of his new reign.

Jesus well knew the mistaken feelings and expectations with which their hearts were filled. He desired to correct them by preaching to them the real truths and objects of his mission, yet so as not to excite a violent opposition. Ascending therefore a mountain, he sat down for the purpose of teaching, and his disciples gathered round him. They hoped to hear him speak of his kingdom; they perhaps expected that he was about to assume to himself its dignities, and raise the standard of deliverance. He did speak to them of his kingdom; but it was a spiritual, not a temporal kingdom. He did proclaim deliverance; not, however, from the Roman yoke, as they were desiring, but from superstition, false doctrine, and sin. Who are they, said he, that shall inherit this new kingdom of God? The great men of the land? the prosperous, the proud, the aspiring, those that are thirsty for revenge, those that are girding on the armor for battle? I tell you No! It is the poor in spirit, the humble, the merciful, the meek, the peace-makers, the pure in heart; — it is these for whom this kingdom is designed. Such is the doctrine with which he opened his discourse to the listening multitudes; a doctrine calculated to crush their hopes, to disappoint their ambition, to mortify their favorite desires. It was assuring them that they could not find in him such a Messiah as the nation was looking for. It was turning them away from all outward objects of gratification, to find the sources of greatness and happiness in their own souls.

This opening of our Lord's Sermon on the Mount exhibits in its perfection the genius of his religion. It embodies the whole practical spirit of his Gospel. It discloses the real sources of human happiness, the real elements of true virtue. It was uttered with an especial view to the peculiar errors of those whom he addressed; but it equally attacks the most prevalent errors of all periods. It unveils to all men of all times the great but slighted truth, that it is the humble and unassuming, rather than the aspiring and haughty, who enjoy most really the happiness of this world, while they insure that of the world to come.

All the false Messiahs that have ever appeared flattered the prejudices and passions of the people, and exhibited the sort of character which they expected and desired. This is what impostors would naturally attempt to do. Only one that truly came from God would have the wisdom and courage to oppose himself to the favorite opinions of the people, and to claim their allegiance while he was contradicting their cherished notions of what the Christ should be. It is only because Jesus was truly from God, that he was able to rise so wonderfully above all his nation, to extend his views so widely beyond them, and, without any aid from human power, to devise a plan for the moral instruction and religious regeneration of the world, which none of those around him were able fully to comprehend.

The whole discourse, from beginning to end, bore a similar character. It was taken up with correcting the erroneous interpretations of the moral law which prevailed among the people, and in setting forth a higher and purer standard of principle and duty than the scribes and Pharisees taught. He warned his hearers how insufficient is all external form, that the seat of all goodness is the heart, and that no true or acceptable virtue can exist except it originate there. He corrected the errors of their present practice respecting alms-giving, prayer, and fasting. He taught them how to purify these acts from wrong motives, and make them available by simplicity and sincerity. He then taught them how worthless is all worldly and temporal good in comparison of the treasures of a future life; and how unavailing is all anxiety about the prosperity of this world; since there is a kind Providence over all, which, as it forgets not the lily of the field or the sparrow of the air, certainly will not forsake man. He then teaches them the duty of candor and mutual kindness; directs them to cherish a spirit of devout dependence on God, and encourages them to it by the most cheerful promises of his paternal love; admonishes them of the necessity of adhering to the strait and narrow path of duty, and the danger of straying from it; and warns them against the artifices of false teachers, who were likely to appear among them, and lead them astray. He teaches them that such deceivers should be known by their fruits, like evil trees; and concludes with depicting to them, in the strongest terms, the security of those who would adhere to the principles he had been inculcating, and the ruin that must befall those who should despise and neglect them.

When he had finished this discourse, St. Matthew tells us, that "the people were astonished at his doctrine, for he taught them as one having authority, and not as the scribes." Both the substance and the manner of his teaching were new to them. But what particularly struck them was the air of AUTHORITY with which he uttered his great truths, as if he had a right from heaven to dictate and decide. And this circumstance, so full of dignity and power, when considered in connection with his humble origin and appearance, and the intrinsic beauty and excellence of his doctrine, drew toward him their respect and reverence, though his doctrine was so different from what they had been hoping to hear. Yet it is evident, from what afterwards took place, that he had by no means succeeded in correcting their erroneous notions respecting the nature of his office and kingdom.

As he came down from the mountain, he was met by a man diseased with leprosy, — an odious disease, unknown in our country, but common in the East, and an object of great horror. It affects the skin with violent swellings and blotches, and spreads till it corrupts the whole body, and renders the patient an object of disgust to all who behold him. The suffering it occasions is intense. It is also contagious; and therefore the law of Moses separated lepers from all intercourse

Matthew viii. 2. Mark i. 40. Luke v. 12.

with other men. Hence, in cases which were incurable, and such were most cases of long standing, the sufferings and privations of those affected by it were most pitiable. Cut off from society, shunned by all they met, they dragged out a miserable existence, without alleviation and without hope.

It was one of these wretched beings who now threw himself in our Lord's way. Confident that he had power to restore him, he fell on his face, and besought him, "Lord, if thou wilt, thou canst make me clean." The strong faith which was evinced in these words pleased our Lord, and he immediately put forth his hand, and touched him, saying, "I will; be thou clean." And it was so. He stood up a sound and healthy man. Jesus then desired him not to stay and publish the news of his cure, but to go immediately to the priest. For the law respecting the treatment of the leprosy was very particular and rigid [Leviticus xiv.], and required of every one who had been cleansed that he should offer a certain sacrifice at the temple. Jesus did not choose to interfere with the execution of this law; and therefore directed this man to go without delay, and show himself to the priest, and make the offering which Moses commanded.

There is another thing to be observed of this miracle. Jesus commanded the man not to noise it abroad. Now it probably had not been performed in the presence of the multitude; for as a leper was always avoided, no one would choose to be present where he appeared; and it is a proof of the man's earnest faith, that he was able to make his way to our Lord's presence, as well as of our Lord's benevolence, that he would receive and touch a person so odious to all. Being done therefore in private, the cure was not known to the multitude, and Jesus forbade it to be published, because he was already in some degree incommoded by the crowds that followed him, and it was very important that he should not create such a degree of excitement as might give occasion to his enemies to complain of him to the government, and thus shorten the period of his ministry. We read that on several occasions he expressed this desire to conceal his miracles. He wished to avoid all unnecessary occasion of offence, and to complete, without premature interruption, the work given him to do.

Having dismissed the leper, Jesus left the multitude, and retired to a desert place and prayed. His object probably was, both to avoid the throngs of people and give them an opportunity to disperse, and to gain for himself strength and enjoyment from the exercises of devotion. His example teaches us true wisdom, — to retire at times from the excitement of the world, and seek light and truth in communion with our hearts and with God.

CHAPTER IX.

JESUS RETURNS TO CAPERNAUM. — PERFORMS VARIOUS MIRACLES. — CALLS MATTHEW.

How long our Lord had now been absent from Capernaum we cannot tell, nor to what distance he had extended his travels. The account given by the Evangelists is very general, and such as does not render it necessary to suppose the time very long, nor the circuit very great. Capernaum was still his head-quarters; and having escaped from the crowds, who, as Mark intimates, had prevented his entering the city, he returned thither to his home.

As soon as his arrival was known, a Roman centurion, that is, captain of a company of a hundred soldiers, sent to him a message, through the Jewish elders of the city, entreating him to visit and heal a favorite servant of his who was ill of the palsy. The elders seconded the message by giving a high character of this Roman officer, who had gained the good-will of the citizens by his acts of kindness, and especially by

Matthew viii. 6. Mark i. 45. Luke vii. 1.

his munificence in building them a synagogue. Jesus accompanied them; but it shows the modesty and faith of the centurion, that he sent other messengers to meet our Lord and save him the trouble of coming to his house; for I know, said he, that this great prophet, wherever he may be, can as easily command diseases to go and come as I can command my soldiers. Jesus was struck by this union of humility and faith; and, turning to the people who followed, expressed his approbation by declaring, "I say unto you, I have not found so great faith, no, not in Israel." The messengers, on their return to the house, found the servant well.

The next day he went to the city of Nain, accompanied, as Luke says, by his disciples and much people. The distance could not have been far from twenty miles; and as he seems to have returned very shortly to Capernaum, it is not improbable that he made this excursion for the very purpose of working the miracle which he did there. He may have had a particular friendship for the family of the young man who died, as he had for that of Lazarus. However this may have been, he reached Nain just as a funeral procession came out of the gate. It was the funeral of a young man, the only son of a widow, and attended by a great company of people. It

Luke vii. 11.

was a scene to call forth our Lord's sympathy, and he at once approached the weeping mother with a word of consolation. "Weep not," said he; and laying his hand on the bier to arrest the bearers, while the attending multitude stood wondering at the strange interruption, he raised his voice in a few words of authority and power,—"Young man, I say unto thee, arise!" In the sight of all the people the dead arose, and was restored to the arms of his mother. This was done in the presence of hundreds at the city gate, who expressed their admiration by loudly glorifying God, and saying, "A great prophet hath risen up among us, and God hath visited his people." St. Luke remarks, that this event did much to extend his celebrity throughout Judæa. It is the first miracle of the kind recorded. Like the other two instances which afterward occurred, it was accompanied by circumstances of peculiar interest, and such as render it a touching proof of the benevolence of our Saviour's disposition.

After returning to Capernaum, he proposed one evening, in order to escape the multitudes which had collected, to sail over to the other side of the lake. The breadth of this lake is about six miles, and the length nearly eighteen. Much of the scenery about it is beautiful and striking. It is surrounded for the most part by high hills,

Matthew viii. 23. Mark iv. 35. Luke viii. 22.

and in fact lies in a sort of basin formed by two ranges of mountains, which enclose it, except at the northern and southern extremities, where the river Jordan enters and departs. It is, by this means, protected in general from the winds, and rendered for the most part a placid and tranquil sheet of water. Yet it is subject to occasional blasts coming suddenly from the hills, which blow with the fury of a hurricane, and endanger all that is floating on its waves. Such a tempest arose on the night that our Saviour went upon the water. As Luke expresses it, there *came down* a storm of wind from the mountains, and they were filled with water, and were in jeopardy. The affrighted disciples rushed to their master, who was quietly asleep, crying, "Lord, save us; we are perishing!" "Why are you fearful?" said he; "where is your faith?" He arose, and rebuked the wind and the waters, and there was a calm. Much as they had known of his supernatural power, this new exhibition of it occasioned new amazement in the minds of his followers. It filled them with fresh awe, and they expressed their astonishment one to another. "What manner of man is this, that even the winds and the seas obey him!"

They landed on the opposite shore, in the country of Gadara. Gadara was the capital of Peræa,

Matthew viii. 28. Mark v. 1. Luke vii. 26.

as the region on the other side of the Jordan was called, and gave its name to the surrounding country. It was a place of considerable importance in its day, having been rebuilt by Pompey the Great, and being one of the five cities in which the Romans established courts of justice. In the neighborhood was Gergesa, also a considerable city, with an extensive surrounding region attached to it. The lands belonging to the one city were in part included in those of the other, so that they went indifferently by the name of either; which accounts for the circumstance, that Matthew speaks of the Gergesenes, while Mark and Luke speak of the Gadarenes.

On arriving on this coast, and proceeding toward the city, there came out from the tombs, which in that part of the world are generally built outside of the city walls, two demoniacs, or men possessed with demons. These persons, like raving and unmanageable madmen, lived among the tombs. One of them was so fierce and dangerous, that it had been found impossible to keep him confined; he broke away from the chains in which he was bound, and raged wildly abroad, being night and day in the mountains and among the tombs, howling, and cutting himself with stones. The description answers precisely to that of a raving maniac; and, indeed, many learned men are of opinion that to be "possessed with a demon" is only another mode of expressing the loss of reason, and other deplorable disorders. When the ancients, the heathens as well as the Jews, witnessed the wild conduct and speech of men who were beside themselves, they attributed it to some evil spirit, or demon, which had taken possession of their bodies. When they met a person crazed, or lunatic, or subject to epileptic attacks, they accounted for the disorder by saying that a demon had possessed him. Just as when the Jews at Jerusalem heard Jesus accuse them of a purpose to put him to death, and use language which they did not comprehend, they said, "Thou hast a demon, and art mad." It is probable that this is the truth in regard to the demoniacs mentioned in the New Testament. Many learned men, however, think otherwise, and suppose that the persons spoken of were really possessed by unclean spirits. This is not the place to decide the question. Whichever opinion we may adopt, the miracles which Jesus so often wrought for their relief and cure were among the most signal and beneficent of his ministry, and seem to have been esteemed by the people of that day as among the most decisive proofs of supernatural power. They are equally so, whether we regard them as driving from the body a foul spirit which had usurped a lodging there, or restoring to it the understanding which had departed. None but a power which came from God could be equal to either.

The other of the two demoniacs who met Jesus was probably of a milder character, and therefore is overlooked in the account given by Mark and Luke. Matthew mentions both. And all three alike give the particulars of the miracle which our Saviour wrought for their cure. It is one of the most remarkable in its circumstances of any that are recorded in the New Testament. The poor maniac, who fancied himself possessed by a legion of foul spirits, and sometimes spake in their name and sometimes in his own, entreated Jesus to send them out into a herd of swine that was feeding hard by. It has been thought difficult to explain why our Lord should give assent to so mad a request; for the consequence was, that the whole herd rushed precipitately down the banks of the lake and were destroyed. This fearful exhibition of power struck awe into the beholders, and satisfied both them and the patient himself, beyond doubt, that he was thoroughly cured of his disease, — which was probably the object our Lord had in view. The inhabitants of the country seem to have been filled with consternation at the occurrence. They crowded about him, entreating him to leave their coasts, and he accordingly departed. The man whom he had restored to his right mind begged to accompany him, in testimony of his gratitude and devotion. But Jesus would not permit it. He enjoined on him to remain in his own land, and publish there the goodness of God. He accordingly did so; and was the means of spreading the knowledge of Jesus on that side the Jordan. This circumstance proves that when our Saviour forbade any one to publish his miracles, it was for some peculiar local or temporary reasons.

Our Lord's return to Capernaum was welcomed by the people, who were waiting for him, and who immediately thronged about him as before. They followed him to his house, and assembled there in such numbers that there was no room to receive them, no, not so much as about the door. Luke observes, that at this time there were present Pharisees and doctors of the law from all parts of Galilee and Judæa, and even from Jerusalem. It is not improbable, that they had arrived at Capernaum, during his absence, and that this was in part the occasion of the great pressure at this time. They sat with him in the court, or central square of the house, while the people stood crowding around, and filled the adjoining apartments as well as the passage-way from the street. The Jewish houses were built in the form of a hollow square; the court in the middle was the usual place of sitting and receiving company, and the

Matthew ix. 1. Mark ii. 1. Luke v. 17.

various apartments for the use of the family opened into it on every side. The square was usually paved with stone or marble, on which were laid mats or carpeting, and an awning was stretched overhead, as a protection from the weather.

While Jesus was thus sitting in the court, discoursing with the Pharisees, the doctors, and the people, a company arrived at the street door bringing a man sick of the palsy. But they found it impossible to get near. Even the passageway and the space about the street door were thronged. They were not, however, discouraged; and as they could not gain admittance in the usual way, they resolved to try another. They carried the poor man up to the roof of the house. This might have been done by means of the stairs which are placed in the entrance from the street, except that the crowd seems to have been too great to allow of access to them. They therefore probably entered a neighboring house, ascended the stairway, and walked from house to house along the roofs, which in the East are flat, and generally communicate with one another. Having thus reached the spot over the head of our Lord, they took away a portion of the balustrade, and the awning which covered the court, and let down the bed of the invalid directly at the Saviour's side.

He perceived at once the earnest faith which had prompted such an extraordinary act, and in a tone of kindness said, "Son, be of good cheer; thy sins be forgiven thee." It was a prevalent opinion among the Jews that bodily disorders were the consequences of sin. Perhaps Jesus knew that such was the fact in the present instance, and intended to remind the sick man of his faults, while he gave assurance of compassion. His words were indeed equivalent to an assurance that he should be healed. But it was a new mode of expression. The people had not heard it from him before; and some of the scribes and Pharisees who were present murmured at it. They thought it blasphemous. Jesus, perceiving what passed in their minds, answered them aloud. He told them, that whether he pronounced the forgiveness of sin, or wrought a miracle, it was all one; both alike were demonstrations of his divine mission, and the one as easy as the other; but, that they might know that he had this authority to forgive, he would remove the disease, and thus prove that the sin was forgiven. He accordingly commanded the sick man to rise and walk. He immediately did so, — to the discomfiture of these cavillers, and to the great admiration and joy of the people, who glorified God and were filled with fear, saying, "We never saw it on this fashion."

When we thus repeatedly read of the exclamations of astonishment uttered by those who witnessed our Lord's wonderful works, we must remember that they are not the same company of persons in all cases. Every miracle was doubtless performed in the presence of many who had not witnessed one before. Jesus had now been for some time resident at Capernaum; the inhabitants were familiar with him, and it is not they who would thus throng his house and be amazed at his works. They were undoubtedly strangers, who had come from other places to see with their own eyes the wonders of which they had heard. It is such that were impatiently waiting for him on his return from Gadara, and formed the company that crowded his dwelling; as we have already remarked concerning the Pharisees and doctors from Jerusalem. It is probable, also, that the paralytic was brought from some other place. All the circumstances indicate that he and his friends were strangers at Capernaum. Their impatience and eagerness are not like those of persons dwelling in the same town, who could have access to Jesus every day; but rather of persons who have just arrived from a distance, and cannot rest until their errand is accomplished. This being so, we understand fully the feelings with which the witnesses exclaimed, "We never saw it on this fashion!" If they had been citizens of Capernaum, it would not have been true.

Shortly after this, Jesus went forth again to the side of the lake, and addressed the people there; as he did in several instances. At this time, in passing by the receipt of customs (the booth or office at which the taxes were collected, probably from the vessels which traded at Capernaum), he saw Levi, the publican, who was also named Matthew, sitting there upon duty, and called upon him to follow him. Matthew accordingly did so. As he resided in the same town, he was undoubtedly already well known to our Lord; it is not probable that Jesus would in this way summon any one whom he had not previously known. So it had been in the instances of Andrew and Peter. The Evangelist does not state that Jesus had met them before he saw them at the lake; yet we learn from John's Gospel, that he had previously known them in Judæa. So also he had undoubtedly been acquainted with Matthew, and at this moment only intimated to him that the time was come when he must be devoted exclusively to his service. Matthew accordingly abandoned his office. On occasion of doing so, he made a great feast at his own house, which shows him to have been a man of some consideration and property, to which he invited Jesus,

Matthew ix. 9. Mark ii. 13. Luke v. 27.

and many of his brother publicans, and other guests.

The publicans were officers employed by the Romans for the purpose of collecting the revenues and taxes. They were more odious than tax-gatherers ordinarily are, because they were mostly underlings in office, and the oppressive extortions of underlings are proverbial. There was another reason for the dislike borne them by the Jews, namely, that they were, for the most part, their own countrymen, who were thought to be aiding foreigners in the oppression of their native land. Some upright and honorable men there undoubtedly were among them. Such was Zacchæus, of whom we shall read by and by; and such was Matthew; and we are informed that there was a greater readiness among men of this class to receive the teachings of Jesus than among the higher and more favored classes. Matthew probably invited them to meet Jesus at his table, in order that they might have an opportunity to converse with him, and thus perhaps be brought, like himself, to acknowledge him. It was evidently in the hope that he might benefit them, that Jesus accepted the invitation, as appears by the answer which he made to the Pharisees. These troublesome spies, who seem at this time to have come up from Jerusalem on purpose to watch him, complained of him for eating with publicans and sinners. They intended thus to excite the prejudices of the people. Jesus answered them, that he associated with them in order to do them good. The more they were sinners, the more they needed to be called to repentance. The righteous had no need of him; it was these very sinners that required him. "They that are whole need not a physician, but they that are sick."

When he had justified himself on this point, he was immediately assailed on another. In that age, as in all others, but perhaps in that more than in others, great stress was laid on the external forms of religion, on observances and ceremonies. The Pharisees, who were a leading sect, distinguished themselves by their strictness in these particulars. They were strict in their fasts and solemn in their demeanor, and contrived to impress on the people an idea of their superior sanctity. John the Baptist, also, had practised, and had taught his disciples to practise, severe mortification of body. Jesus encouraged in his followers none of this external austerity. He taught them that religion is an inward affection and a principle of holy living; he required of them to regulate their hearts and their lives, but imposed on them no mere forms. This afforded an obvious objection to his doctrine; and some of John's followers took the present occasion to ask him how it happened, that, while they observed frequent occasions of fasting and solemn prayer, he and his disciples observed none. Jesus answered them, that he regarded fasting as an expression of sadness and mourning; that it would be an unbecoming thing in his disciples, who had no reason to mourn so long as he, their Master, was with them; it would be time enough for them to fast when he should be withdrawn from them. Besides, it would be as incongruous to annex such a mere form to a religious system like his, as it would be to put new wine into old leathern bottles, or to piece an old garment with new cloth. Antiquated forms in a new religion would be only injurious. The bottle must be adapted to the wine, and the form to the system, or they cannot endure.

While thus engaged, one of the rulers of the synagogue, named Jairus, came to him, and, falling down at his feet, entreated him to come and save his dying daughter. The confidence which was felt in his power is very strongly evinced by the manner in which this respectable man addressed him: "Come, and lay thy hand on her, and she shall live." Jesus immediately arose, and proceeded toward the house, followed by a multitude of the people.

As he passed through the streets, another example occurred of the extraordinary confidence of the people in his divine power. A poor woman, who for twelve years had been grievously diseased, and had tried every remedy in vain, said to herself, "If I can but touch his garment, I shall be whole." She did so, and was healed; and Jesus commended her faith in presence of the multitude.

On arriving at the house of Jairus, he was met by all the demonstrations of mourning which customarily attended a Jewish death. He found a crowd of people lamenting, and the hired minstrels bewailing, and altogether what Mark calls a "tumult." He immediately put them all out, and suffered none others to enter with him the dwelling of affliction and death but Peter, James, and John, who on this, as on certain other occasions, were selected as the witnesses of his more private hours. With them and the parents of the deceased child, he proceeded to the room where she lay, spoke the word, and she returned to life.

This is the second miracle of raising the dead recorded by the Evangelists. It is remarkable that, out of the multitudes thus restored, only three instances are specified in the history; and it is pleasing to find in each of them a circumstance of peculiarly tender interest, which may help to explain the reason of their selection. By the first, an only son was restored to the arms of a widowed mother; by the second, an only daughter was

Matthew ix. 18. Mark v. 22. Luke viii. 41.

given back to her disconsolate parents; and by the third, a brother, an only brother there is rea son to believe, was restored to his fond and confiding sisters. It is delightful thus to see our affectionate Lord carry his divine power into the circles of private and domestic life, and in a manner consecrate the pure relationship of home. A prophet might have displayed his power in a thousand ways even more striking than these; but what sympathy and kind-heartedness must have belonged to him who chose occasions on which he could most signally bless the children while he glorified the Father!

On the same day, Jesus gave sight to two blind men, who came to him in the street as he returned from the house of Jairus, and restored speech to a dumb man who was thought to be possessed of a demon. The Pharisees, meantime, still hung around his path. They would probably have interfered at the raising of the young girl, if they had been admitted to the house. They now cavilled again, and suggested for the first time an explanation of the miracles they witnessed, of which they afterwards made great use. "He casteth out demons," they said, "through the prince of the demons."

It is apparent that the events of this day are recorded with unusual minuteness. There is no good reason, however, for supposing it any other than a fair example of the manner in which the days of Jesus were usually spent. It is possible that the great dinner given by Matthew on resigning his office as publican may have caused the several events connected with it to leave a more distinct impression, and to be therefore more particularly recorded. But what an idea does it give of the activity and benevolence of our Lord's ministry, to remember that such a day, thus crowded with acts of kindness and wisdom, was not remarkable above other days for the works it contained!

CHAPTER X.

THE OPPOSITION OF THE PHARISEES TO JESUS. — HIS TREATMENT OF THEM.

IN the last chapter we had occasion to notice the circumstance that many Pharisees and doctors of the law had visited Capernaum for the purpose of conversing with and watching Jesus. The instances there given of the vexatious spying and cavilling by which they endeavored to perplex and thwart him are but specimens of what was frequently occurring. It may help us to understand the opposition with which our Saviour had to contend, and exalt our idea of the magnanimity and meekness with which he endured it, to collect under one view the various incidents of this nature which are recorded by the Evangelists. To many of them no definite mark is affixed by which we may ascertain when or where they occurred. They are principally related by Luke, whose Gospel, through a large part of it, is a collection of discourses and incidents, thrown together without any pretence of chronological arrangement.* The present is a fitting place for noticing several of these portions of history.

From the time that the Pharisees first took offence at our Lord's teaching and baptizing in Judæa, they pursued him with unremitting hostility. It was probably owing to their influence at Jerusalem that he was prevented from exercising his ministry in that city. Even at the festivals, his visits had been interrupted and cut short by opposition and open assault. They pursued him into the country. Wherever he was, there were scribes and Pharisees; wherever he went, they followed him. And we are reconciled to the petty persecution and unprincipled calumny with which they harassed him, only by observing that they thus furnished opportunities for some of his most delightful instructions, and served to display in constantly new forms the wisdom and loveliness of his character.

In several instances he was invited to dine at the houses of these arrogant but distinguished men. It is reasonable to suppose that this was sometimes done from motives of real respect; but sometimes, also, from very different motives. It seems rarely to have happened that some one pres-

* Chapters xi.-xviii. The "order" spoken of in Ch. i. 3, is not the order of time.

Luke vii. 36.

ent at such seasons did not take the occasion to cavil or insult; and the issue always was to bring forth a new illustration of his doctrines and character.

One of the most affecting incidents of his life occurred on one of these occasions. As he was dining with a Pharisee, a woman of the city, whose name is not given, and of whom nothing is told except that she was a sinner, entered the apartment where they sat, for the purpose of doing him an act of honor. She brought with her an alabaster box of precious ointment, such, probably, as it was customary to use for the purpose of anointing the head on occasions of special ceremony. She went behind the guests, who, instead of *sitting* at the table as we do, were reclined at full length on couches, leaning on their left arms. She thus approached the extended feet of Jesus, intending to pour upon them this costly perfume. So profusely did she weep from the fulness of her feelings, that Luke expresses it by saying, "she bathed his feet with her tears." She wiped them with the hair of her head, kissed them, and poured on them the fragrant preparation.

The Pharisee was scandalized at the scene, and said within himself, "If this man were a prophet, he would have known that this woman is a sinner." It was not in the heart of the Pharisees to have sympathy or forbearance for those whom they regarded as sinners. They esteemed themselves to be righteous, and despised others. But Jesus was full of compassion for them, especially in their penitence; and he never appears more amiable and heavenly than in the reply which he made at this time to the thought of the Pharisee. He gently, but pungently, reproved the spirit which actuated him, and vindicated the claim of the sinful to compassionate regard. "Her sins, which are many, are forgiven," said he, "for she hath loved much." And then turning to the weeping woman, he said, "Thy sins are forgiven." Some of the company began to murmur at this; but, without taking notice of it, he added, "Thy faith hath saved thee; go in peace."

We remark here, by the way, that this difference between the manner in which Jesus, and that in which the Jewish leaders, felt toward sinners and treated them, illustrates one of the characteristic distinctions of his life. Without any greater lenity toward crime, and with unspeakably higher notions of moral purity, he united a sympathy for the unhappy delinquents, and a compassionate tenderness towards them, altogether foreign from the supercilious hardness of the self-righteous Pharisees. He was touched with a feeling of their infirmities, and never shunned them when he could be in the way of doing them good. Yet this beautiful circumstance was perverted into a ground of accusation against him. "He eateth and drinketh with publicans and sinners," it was said; "he receiveth sinners, and eateth with them"; "he is a friend of publicans and sinners." To these accusations, which were intended to cast obloquy on him in the minds of the people, he replied, that his very object was to seek and save that which was lost; to call, not the righteous, but sinners to repentance. And on one occasion he enlarged on this thought, and went on, in several parables of most affecting beauty, to picture forth the unchanging and impartial love of the God who had sent him, and the inexhaustible fulness of his mercy. One of these was the parable of the Prodigal Son,—so familiarly known, so universally admired, so full of delightful consolation and encouragement to the humble and fearful penitent. Nothing could be more opposed to the principles of the proud Pharisee, and nothing more characteristic of the spirit of Christ and his Gospel.

On another occasion a Pharisee, with whom he was dining, expressed surprise that he had not washed before sitting down,—a negligence which he, with his scrupulous observance of forms and ablutions, accounted as nothing less than a sin. This led Jesus to remark on the folly of laying so much stress on outward appearances and merely

Luke xi. 37, xv.

mechanical observances, to the neglect of inward purity and important duties. And when a lawyer in the company interrupted him, he extended his reproof to that class of men also. This brought upon him a general attack from the scribes and Pharisees present, who urged him vehemently, and incited him to speak on many subjects; lying in wait for him, says Luke, and hoping that he would let something fall which might be matter of accusation against him. It excites our admiration of his wisdom, that he was always able to avoid the snares which they thus laid for him.

On a certain Sabbath he dined with one of the chief Pharisees, when the very purpose seemed to be to watch him. This he perceived, but would not let it stand in the way of his benevolence. There was in the company a dropsical person, whom he desired to restore to health. And as he had had experience of the malicious construction which these men put on his Sabbath-day charities, he turned to them, and asked, "Is it lawful to heal on the Sabbath day?" They did not choose to answer the question, but it prevented their opposition at the time. It was on this same occasion, that, unappalled by the presence of a company assembled around him as spies, he remarked freely on the ambitious spirit displayed by many among them, and gave one of his most striking

Luke xiv. 1.

lessons on humility. He then turned to the master of the house, and with the greatest freedom and plainness instructed him concerning real charity and the duty of disinterested kindness; advising him to spread his table, not for his equals and superiors who could honor him in return, but for the friendless and suffering. This would be true happiness; for though *they* could not reward their benefactor, he should be recompensed at the resurrection of the just. So impossible was it for Jesus to regard man as any other than an immortal being! One of the company, affected by his holy words, remarked, in a tone different from that in which the feast began, "Happy are they that shall eat bread in the kingdom of God!" Upon this hint, our Lord proceeded to recite that parable, so full of direct and solemn admonition, which describes those who would not come to the offered supper, and whose places were therefore filled by persons whom they despised. The tone and purpose of the parable are such as to indicate that this scene took place toward the close of his ministry.

The Sabbath was one of those subjects to which these rigid formalists often recurred in their accusations of Jesus. The liberty which he allowed to himself and his followers on that day seemed to them profane. He was obliged to defend him-

Matthew xii. 1. Mark ii. 23. Luke vi. 1.

self and his disciples for plucking and eating a few ears of corn as they passed through the fields. On this occasion it was that he stated his doctrine on the subject in these emphatic words: "The Sabbath was made for man, and not man for the Sabbath; therefore the Son of man is Lord also of the Sabbath."

But what is yet more remarkable, and shows strikingly both their superstition and their enmity, he was obliged to defend even his miracles against this charge of Sabbath-breaking. It was his healing a man on the Sabbath which formed the pretence for the first violent assault on him in Jerusalem. The same circumstance was alleged against him when he healed the man born blind, at the feast of Pentecost. So far was this irrational opposition carried, that when he had done an act of benevolence in the synagogue on that day, the ruler of the synagogue cried out to the people, with great displeasure: "There are six days in which men ought to work; in these, therefore, come and be healed, and not on the Sabbath day." "Thou hypocrite," said Jesus; "doth not each of you on the Sabbath loose his ox or his ass from the stall, and lead him away to water? And ought not this woman, being a daughter of Abraham, whom Satan hath bound,

John v. 9, ix. Luke xiii. 10. Matthew xii. 9.
Mark iii. 1. Luke vi. 6.

lo, these eighteen years, be loosed from this bond on the Sabbath day?" At this reply, all his adversaries were ashamed, says Luke; as well they might be. On another occasion, when he knew that the Pharisees were watching him, he put the same question before doing the miracle; and when they made him no reply, it is not strange that "he looked round on them with indignation, being grieved at the hardness of their hearts." What more likely to give indignant grief to a pure and benevolent mind, than to perceive the best actions misconstrued and perverted by bitter and malignant prejudice? Instead of allowing themselves to be convinced, the Pharisees thought only of revenge; and went out and held a council against him.

It was through such opposition as this, gratuitous and unprincipled, that our Lord was compelled to pursue his trying way. Perhaps it was never more disheartening than when these men attributed his miracles to Beelzebub, the prince of the demons. That he wrought the miracles, they could not deny; but, instead of allowing in them the hand of God, they chose to explain them away by attributing them to demoniacal power. This argued an obstinacy in unbelief, a determined hardness of heart, which must render them incapable of being convinced. It was the highest

Matthew xii. 22. Mark iii. 19. Luke xi. 14.

degree of wilful blindness and depravity. Therefore, after showing how absurd it was to suppose that the evil spirits would furnish him with power to destroy themselves, he went on to show the hopelessness of that mind which could make such a suggestion. If they had spoken against himself, he said, it would have been pardonable; but to ascribe his miraculous works to evil spirits, and thus despise the Divine agency which was manifest in them, was an offence which could not be forgiven.

It aggravated the sin, and rendered it a greater grief to the feeling mind of Jesus, that these men were at the same time calling upon him to show them some sign. "Master, we would see a sign from thee." As if all his wonderful works had not been sign enough; as if they were willing to believe, provided he would only give them sufficient evidence. To such calls for evidence, made in such a spirit, he had but one reply. It was such a reply as their perverseness and hypocrisy deserved. He referred them, darkly, under the image of Jonah in the fish, to his future burial and resurrection; and proceeded to upbraid in severe terms their incredulity and impenitence.

When we thus observe the manner and spirit in which these men set themselves in opposition to our Lord, we are not surprised that he often spoke of them with severity, and took pains to unmask them to the people. He did this even at their own tables. He rebuked them and expostulated with them to their faces. He exposed them in their true character to the people. He directed against them many of his most solemn parables. And in expressing his abhorrence of their hollow-heartedness, pride, and oppression, all indulged under the sanctimonious appearance of religion, he used words of indignation which on no other occasion escaped his gentle lips.

CHAPTER XI.

SECOND TOUR THROUGH GALILEE. — THE TWELVE APOSTLES APPOINTED. — JOHN'S MESSAGE TO JESUS. — JESUS GOES UP TO THE FEAST OF DEDICATION AT JERUSALEM.

WE return to the regular train of the narrative. Jesus had passed but few days in Capernaum and its vicinity, when he left it for the purpose of making another circuit among the towns and villages of Galilee. This was probably in a different direction from the former, and he was differently accompanied. With the increased attention which had been drawn to his ministry, the number of his devoted friends and permanent attendants had been constantly augmenting; and when he now started forth on an excursion through the country, we find him not only accompanied, as before, by a promiscuous crowd, but by persons of rank and name. Among these were several female friends, who, it is said, "ministered to him of their substance," and through whose kind attentions and charities he and his disciples were enabled to

Matthew ix. 35. Luke viii. 1.

devote themselves to their work without anxiety. On the part of these ladies, this seems to have been the offering of gratitude for the exercise of his miraculous power in their behalf. They had been "healed by him of evil spirits and infirmities." To Mary Magdalene he had been a peculiar benefactor. Joanna was the wife of Herod's steward; probably, therefore, a person of some consequence. Of Susanna and the others nothing special is known. But the names of these faithful friends, who sought to promote the comfort of their benefactor during his laborious life, who forsook him not when in shame and suffering, and who affectionately watched at his tomb, deserve to be recorded to their everlasting honor. They could not go abroad and preach his Gospel, like Peter and James; but they did what they could, while he lived and when he died, with tender and persevering fidelity. They gave him their time, their property, their affections, and their tears; and they have put to shame the coldness of many among his modern followers, who know more of his real glory than they did, and yet are backward to sacrifice anything in his cause.

It was about this time, either just before commencing this new journey, or soon after its commencement, that he selected from among his dis-

Matthew x. 1. Mark iii. 13. Luke vi 12.

ciples the twelve apostles. This was a great and important step. He needed assistants in his ministry, for he was unable to go everywhere himself, and yet it was important that many places should be visited. He knew, too, that he should continue to labor but a short time, and that it was necessary to make provision for carrying on and completing his work after he should be taken away. Having this object in view, Luke tells us that he retired to a mountain to pray, and continued all night in prayer to God. When it was morning, he called together the disciples, and from among them chose twelve, — undoubtedly men who had been acquainted with him, and whom he thoroughly knew. Four of them — Andrew, Peter, John, and Philip — had been attached to him from the very beginning of his ministry, and the first James from an early period. Matthew was, like himself, a citizen of Capernaum. The other six are not named in the Gospels until now. Two of them, Thomas the incredulous and Judas the traitor, became conspicuous in the history of their Master's life. James, the son of Alpheus, and Thaddeus, or Judas, his brother, were afterwards distinguished as writers of Epistles. The other two are less known. Their names were Bartholomew and Simon.

These are the men who devoted their lives to Christ, and through whom his religion was preserved and spread. Doubtless they felt themselves honored by the distinction conferred upon them; but they little understood its true nature. It is evident that at this time, and long after, instead of comprehending that Jesus was only a religious teacher, establishing a religious empire, they thought him preparing the way for a secular kingdom. It was nothing strange, in their view, that he should devote himself to religious teaching; for the whole history of their people was religious. David had been at once a prophet and a warrior. There was no distinction in their minds between the church and the commonwealth; and the Messiah, who was to renew the one, would necessarily plead for the other. It did not help, therefore, to undeceive the people or the disciples, that Jesus was occupied as a religious teacher. They perhaps thought it the most politic course to be pursued, until he should have collected adherents in sufficient numbers to maintain his ground steadfastly. When we read the instructions given to the Twelve as they went forth, we can hardly realize that they should not have perceived their error. Yet their subsequent history abundantly proves that they did not. It happened with them as has often happened with others, — their state of mind colored what they heard, and enabled them to put upon it such an interpretation as they liked. And it is no more strange that they found their own notions favored by their Lord's teachings, than that Christians of every variety of faith have found their own peculiar views written in the Scriptures.

In giving them their commission, our Lord, first of all, endowed them with the power of working miracles, that it might be known at once, wherever they went, that they were sent out by him, and that the kingdom of God was at hand. Their mighty works were to be their credentials. He commanded them to limit their visit to their own countrymen, to carry nothing with them on their journey, to use conciliating manners to all, yet to be prepared for opposition, persecution, and even death. The closing passages of his charge were impressive and awful in the highest degree, and must have made those humble men feel that they were accepting a mission of the most fearful responsibility, for which their lives and habits had ill prepared them, and which they could hope to sustain only by a reliance on the Divine power which Jesus promised for their aid. What must have been the emotions of that moment, when they found themselves removed from their obscure occupations and mechanical employments, to take up the sacred office of prophet, to go out as messengers of the glorious Messiah, and, amid obloquy and peril, summon the nation to its allegiance! Clothed with the power of miracles, commanded to do good and to proclaim repentance and the coming of the Messiah, they departed to begin their work, — a work whose true object they knew not, which is still going on, and which is to cease only when all men in all lands have received the tidings which they spread.

To the mind of Jesus only was the full grandeur of this undertaking known. He alone knew that he was commencing an enterprise never before imagined by man, — the regeneration and salvation of the human race. It was the consciousness of this, and his knowledge of the resolution, faith, and self-sacrifice requisite for the task, which imparted such solemn earnestness to the warnings and appeals with which he introduced the Twelve to their share of the work; and which, we may believe, had led him to consecrate the previous night to solitary prayer on the mountain.

This important step having been taken, Jesus proceeded on his second tour through Galilee. In what direction he went, through what places he passed, how long he was thus occupied, and what were the works he did, are matters which have not been recorded by the Evangelists.

It seems to have been during this tour that he received a message from John the Baptist. John had been now for some time in prison; and, hearing there a report of the wonderful things done

Matthew xi. 2. Luke vii. 18.

by Jesus, seems to have thought it strange that he, the Messiah, should not do something for his deliverance. He not improbably expected that he would come and rescue him. Perhaps, too, he wondered that he continued peaceably to preach, without assuming the state and power of his office. As he brooded over these thoughts in the confinement of his dungeon, he might even come to doubt whether after all this was the real Messiah. At any rate, he wished to convey to him a rebuke for leaving his forerunner to suffer, when he could so easily deliver him. He therefore sent to him two of his disciples to put the question to him plainly, — "Art thou he that should come, or do we look for another?"

The two disciples came, and delivered their message. It happened that at that time Jesus was occupied with the people who attended him, and he went on doing his mighty works without replying to what had been said. When he had finished, he turned to the messengers, and bade them go back and tell John what they had seen him do; — this would be a sufficient answer to his inquiry; and he added, with something of reproof, that it would be happy for him if he did not allow his own personal feelings of disappointment to create doubt in his mind concerning him.

But though he thought it necessary to send to John a message somewhat severe, no sooner had the disciples departed, than he turned to the people, and in earnest language pronounced a eulogy upon him; praising his firmness and self-denial, and declaring him the greatest of the prophets. From this, he passed to censure the inconsistency of the people, who rejected John for his austerity, and yet condemned himself for his indulgence. He then uttered his severe and thrilling denunciation against Chorazin, Bethsaida, and Capernaum, because, having witnessed so much of his miracles and his ministry, they yet had not repented and reformed. But his compassionate mind could not pause here. He burst forth in loud praise to God for the gracious wisdom with which he had revealed himself, not to the wise of this world, but to the simple; and he ended with that affectionate invitation to receive him and his doctrine, which it is impossible in certain states of mind to read without tears. "Come unto me, all ye that labor and are heavy laden, and I will give you rest. Take my yoke upon you, and learn of me, for I am meek and lowly in heart, and ye shall find rest to your souls. For my yoke is easy and my burden is light."

In these labors and excursions, the autumn was now far advanced, and the feast of Dedication was approaching. This was not an appointed festival of the law, and therefore it was not binding on the people to attend it. Our Lord, however, proposed to be present at its celebration; and therefore, instead of returning home to Capernaum, he took the road to Jerusalem. At this time it probably was that he went through Samaria, and fell in with the ten lepers near a certain town, who besought him to heal them, and only one of whom, a Samaritan, returned to express his gratitude. The exclamation which Jesus made on the occasion is eminently characteristic and touching. "Were there not ten cleansed?" said he; "but where are the nine? There are none returned to give glory to God, save this stranger." The nine Jews made no acknowledgment for the blessing.

Now also it probably was, that, when arrived at Bethany, within about two miles of Jerusalem, he visited the family of Martha and Mary. Martha, little understanding his true character, made great exertions to provide an entertainment for the distinguished guest; and when she found Mary wholly taken up with listening to his conversation, she went so far as even to complain to him, that she was left to attend to the family concerns alone, and begged him to direct her sister to help her. Our Lord replied in those memorable words, so often quoted since,—"Martha, Martha, thou art careful and troubled about many things; but one

Luke xvii. 11. Luke x. 38.

thing is needful; and Mary hath chosen that good part which shall not be taken away from her." It was attention to his instructions, not to himself, which he desired.

From Bethany he proceeded to Jerusalem, and arrived there in the midst of the feast of the Dedication. This festival occurred in the beginning of winter. It was instituted by Judas Maccabæus in commemoration of the cleansing of the temple, after it had been profaned by Antiochus Epiphanes. It seems to have become one of the favorite solemnities of the nation; being kept with great pomp for eight days, during which time the sacrifices were multiplied, the houses were illuminated, and the rejoicing of the people was testified by a variety of diversions and music. It was sometimes called the feast of Lights.

The people thronged the courts of the temple, as at the other festivals; and there Jesus appeared amongst them, walking in Solomon's porch, — the piazza, it is thought, which extended along the eastern side of the Court of the Gentiles. It was about ten weeks since he had last been seen there. Then he had been beset by enemies, and driven from the temple in fear of his life. Since that time he had been in a distant part of the country, active in teaching the people, gathering his followers, appointing his assistants, seeming to claim the

John x. 22.

Messiahship, yet not openly declaring himself, and by no means assuming the appearance which the Messiah was expected to assume. Therefore the opinions of men were still divided about him, as they had been at his former visits. And when he now returned to them, they immediately came round him, to gain satisfaction to their minds. "How long," said they, "dost thou keep us in doubt? If thou be the Christ, tell us plainly." Now it is clear, that if they had been disposed to believe, the evidence which he had laid before them in his doctrine and miracles was ample. It was because they did not like the character in which he appeared, that they doubted. If he had come in majesty and power, like the princes of the world, denouncing woes on the oppressors of the nation, like Jeremiah, and like the Maccabees, sounding the trumpet and lifting the standard, then they would have believed. It was in vain, therefore, that he attempted to explain himself to them. They were wedded to their own notions; they were fixed in their own prejudices; they would not understand him. They carped at his words; they perverted his meaning; they took up stones once more to stone him; they sought to seize his person. But he again escaped from them; and after having passed, as it appears, less than a day in the city, he quitted it, as if hopeless of doing any good to so conceited and prejudiced a people.

CHAPTER XII.

JESUS RETIRES BEYOND THE JORDAN.—RAISES LAZARUS.—RETURNS TO GALILEE.—HIS PARABLES.—HE VISITS NAZARETH AGAIN.

HAVING thus quitted Jerusalem, our Lord passed over the Jordan, and took up his abode for a time at Bethabara, where John had formerly baptized. Many resorted to him there, and he increased the number of his disciples. It is thought that it was during his residence here that the seventy disciples returned to him. He had sent them out, soon after the twelve apostles and with similar instructions, to preach in the villages. The return of the twelve is nowhere recorded, nor is anything related of the course or effects of their ministry. Some of them at least, perhaps all of them, were with him at the present time; but when they joined him is not said. The return of the seventy is particularly mentioned by Luke, but he gives no history of what they had done, or where they had been. He simply states, that they came to their Master "with joy," especially

John x. 40. Luke x. 17.

exulting that the demons were subject to them in his name. Jesus sympathized in their feeling, and cried out, "I beheld Satan as lightning fall from heaven"; thus expressing the rapidity with which the dominion of evil and sin was falling before the spread of his truth. He added, that he had given them power to effect this great work, in spite of all opposition, and to triumph over all enemies. Then, knowing how easily their pride might be excited by this distinction, he cautioned them not to boast themselves in the possession of miraculous power, but to count it their true cause of joy, that their names were written in heaven.

"In that hour," says Luke, "Jesus rejoiced in spirit," and broke out into a loud thanksgiving. It is the only instance in which he is said to have exhibited an emotion of this nature. It is a solitary example, in the midst of a life of anxiety and toil, of his giving way to a feeling of gladness and exultation. The story of his humble followers, recounting their labors and animated by success, seems to have brought up to his mind a vision of the great and joyful triumph which should hereafter attend the preaching of his truth. He caught a glimpse of that glorious result, which was to compensate all his toil. It cheered him under the recollection of his late rejection at

Jerusalem, and led him to congratulate his disciples, saying, " Blessed are the eyes which see the things which ye see."

While Jesus remained at Bethabara, he received a message from the sisters in Bethany, informing him of the illness of his friend Lazarus. The affectionate intimacy existing between the Saviour and this family is touchingly indicated in the words of the message he received, — " Lord, behold, *he whom thou lovest* is sick." And the Evangelist John, who was doubtless with his Master at this time, adds, that " Jesus loved Martha, and her sister, and Lazarus." Still, though he knew that they had sent to him with the desire that he should come to them, he for two days remained where he was, and left them to their anxiety. He would willingly do anything for them, but he meditated some greater good than their immediate relief. It is often the order of Providence to inflict suffering for a time, in order to prepare the way for blessing. So these sisters were left to mourn, that they might the more rejoice.

To the great surprise of his disciples, our Lord at length proposed to go back to Judæa. What, said they, when the Jews so lately attempted your life, will you unwisely return and put yourself in their power ? But when they learned that Lazarus was dead, they readily consented to accompany him; and it is worth remarking, that it was Thomas, the disciple afterwards so slow to credit his resurrection, who now expressed in strong terms the devoted affection they bore their Master. "Let us go too," said he, "that we may die with him." If the Jews stone him, we will share his fate.

They left Bethabara, crossed the Jordan, and proceeded toward Bethany. He might have raised Lazarus while at a distance, as he had healed the centurion's son at Capernaum. But he preferred to take the long journey (the distance was about thirty miles), because he designed to glorify God and establish his own claims by a signal work; and he would have all its attendant circumstances solemn and striking.

Lazarus had been four days buried when they reached Bethany. It was therefore in the midst of the seven days of mourning, and the friends of the family, from Jerusalem and elsewhere, were with the sisters, making the customary visits of condolence. On hearing of his arrival, Martha rushed out to meet him; but, though overjoyed at his coming, she showed how disappointed and hurt she had been at his neglecting to come sooner. "If thou hadst been here," said she, "my brother had not died." Yet she ventured to hint a hope that he would do something for them. But that she little expected it is evident; for when Jesus kindly hastened to assure her that her brother should rise again, she answered, as if that did not satisfy her, "I know that he will rise again in the resurrection at the last day." Jesus answered her in those sublime and glorious words which are so familiar to our ears, and which must have been wonderful to those who heard them: "I am the resurrection and the life; he that believeth in me, though he were dead, yet shall he live; and whosoever liveth and believeth in me, shall never die." Martha evidently felt these words to the bottom of her soul. She could only reply, that she believed him to be the Messiah; — that one word comprehended everything; and then, as if she had gained all she desired, she went back to the house, and whispered to Mary that the Master had arrived and was waiting for her.

Mary immediately left the house, and accompanied her sister. The friends who were with her followed, thinking that she was going to visit the grave, and all arrived together at the place where Jesus was. Mary threw herself in tears at his feet, and reproached him, as Martha had done, for his tardiness in coming to them. "If thou hadst been here, my brother had not died." The scene was a moving one. When Jesus beheld the two sisters, distressed and in tears, the friends weeping around them, and appealing to him as one who might have helped them, and did not, he could not repress his feelings. He groaned in spirit, and was troubled. He wept, and asked to be conducted to the tomb. The Jews were struck with his sensibility, and said, "Behold how he loved him!" Yet at the same time some of them cavilled, and wondered why, if he could heal a poor blind beggar, he had not saved his friend from death.

The company arrived at the tomb. It was a cave, having the mouth closed with a stone. Our Lord directed that the stone should be removed. Martha, who seems not yet to have suspected what was to take place, objected to this, because it would be offensive. Jesus quietly rebuked her interference: "Said I not, that, if thou wouldst believe, thou shouldst see the glory of God?" The stone was removed. The multitude stood around, looking on, in wondering and silent expectation. And Jesus, whose feelings of sympathy with the mourners had now given way to the joyful confidence that he should at once relieve them, and display the power of God, lifted up his eyes, and uttered a brief thanksgiving,—"Father, I thank thee that thou hast heard me!" This he did that the by-standers might hear him, and be persuaded of his divine mission. Then, with a loud voice, he cried out, "Lazarus, come forth." This was all;—these three simple words; without parade, without pretension, in the simple tone of unquestionable power, he spoke, and the dead man heard him. Enveloped as he was in the garments of death, which were wound close around his body and limbs, he raised himself up from the niche where he was lying in the side of the cave, and stood down upon the floor. Jesus gave directions to loose the raiment which bound him, and he walked out of the cave. We may conjecture the rapture with which the brother and sisters embraced each other, and returned thanks to their friendly deliverer, while they hailed him, with new faith, as the Son of God. Many of the attendant multitude joined them in their acknowledgments, not doubting that he, who had thus raised the dead before their eyes, was indeed the promised and expected one.

Some, however, were of so prejudiced and perverse a mind as to be proof even against this evidence. They went away to inform the Pharisees of what had taken place. A meeting of the Sanhedrim was summoned to discuss the matter. They acknowledged his miracles; indeed, they never had pretended to deny what was so unquestionable; but they reasoned, that this was not the sort of Messiah whom they expected or desired; and that if the people should be brought to maintain his pretensions, it would subject them to the charge of sedition and expose them to the dis-

John xi. 47.

pleasure of the government: "The Romans will come and take away both our place and nation." It was time, therefore, that they should take resolute measures to put a stop to his further progress. And the high priest, Caiaphas, urged them to their bloody purpose, by declaring that it was far better to put one man to death than to run the hazard of this evil to the whole nation. He spoke, says the Evangelist, as high priest, under a divine influence. Little did he imagine that he was urging what, in the mysterious counsels of God, was to promote the glory of the man he strove to destroy, and to hasten the overthrow of the nation he was anxious to save. His counsel prevailed; and from that hour it was resolved that the benevolent prophet of Galilee should die.

Jesus had more than once been exposed to the loss of life from his enemies at Jerusalem, and for that reason had avoided the city, except when called thither by his duty to attend the religious festivals. But now his danger took a new and more formidable aspect. Formerly, it was the Pharisees, the scribes, the populace, who threatened him; now, it was the leading men assembled in solemn council. The sacred Sanhedrim, the venerable Council of Seventy, had decided that he must be put to death. There was no longer any hope that he could escape. But to avoid imme-

John xi. 54.

diate apprehension, and to reserve himself for the Passover when the appointed time for his death would arrive, he immediately withdrew from the vicinity of the city, to a place called Ephraim. How far distant this was, or how large a town, we do not know. It is only said that it was near the wilderness, probably between Jericho and Bethel, and that he resided there some time with his disciples.

From Ephraim he appears to have returned to Galilee; where we again find him, as before, followed by multitudes, as he went about doing good. On one occasion, they so pressed upon him, as he sat in the house, that he was unable even to take his food. The crowd at this time may have been occasioned, in part at least, by an eagerness to hear a discussion relative to his miracles, which was going on between him and some scribes and Pharisees from Jerusalem. The nature of their objection, and the character of his reply, were well adapted to excite the most earnest attention. They have been related in another connection,* and therefore need not be noticed here. But an incident occurred in the midst of the conversation which must not be passed over in silence.

A report of what was going on at the house

Matthew xii. 22. Mark iii. 19. Luke xi. 14.

* Page 123.

reached the ears of the mother and brothers of Jesus, who, it is reasonable to believe, had, like him, left Nazareth and taken up their abode in Capernaum. They anxiously hastened to him; for it was said, "He is beside himself." Finding the crowd so great that they could not gain entrance, they sent in word that they desired to speak with him; hoping in this way to release him from a situation apparently uncomfortable and perhaps perilous. As the word was passed in through the crowd, a woman in the company, hearing his mother named,* cried out, "Blessed is the womb that bare thee!" Happy is the mother of such a son! It was a sudden expression of a natural feeling. But Jesus, who did not wish to have the minds of his hearers diverted from the great subjects on which he was speaking, replied, "Yea, rather blessed are they who hear the word of God and keep it!" Then, stretching out his hand toward his disciples, he added, "Behold my mother and my brothers! For whosoever shall do the will of God, the same is my brother and sister and mother." When this was repeated to his waiting relatives, it must have relieved them from all apprehension. It possibly conveyed to their minds something of a reproof for having allowed themselves to be uneasy about him, and to interrupt him in his duties, when

* [A friend will perceive his own suggestion here.]

they well knew that it was his meat to do his Father's will.

The same day he went out to the side of the lake, accompanied still by a great throng of people. That he might the more advantageously address them, he went on board one of the vessels which lay there, and spoke to them from thence. His discourse at this time was wholly made up of parables; and, if we are right in the arrangement which we have given to the history, it is a curious question, why he commenced this mode of preaching at so late a period of his ministry, and from this time used it so much. For not only the place here assigned to these parables indicates that they were probably the first which he delivered, but the language of the disciples who heard them confirms the supposition. They asked him, "Why speakest thou to them in parables?" as if it were a new thing, a mode of teaching to which they were not accustomed. Does it not seem as if he had become satisfied that the plain, proverbial, perceptive method of instruction hitherto adopted was ineffectual to move and persuade the gross minds of the people? They did not, they would not, understand him. They closed their minds against his true meaning, and avoided the spiritual inferences and applications which he intended they should make. It was in

Matthew xiii. 1. Mark iv. 1. Luke viii. 4.

vain to deal plainly with men pertinaciously resolved against every view but that sensual one of temporal power which engrossed their whole souls. He would therefore change his mode of address. He would speak to the ears they had closed in a corresponding style; he would employ a hidden sense, which would be fully intelligible only to those who came to him with fair and teachable dispositions. To his disciples, therefore, he explained his parables, because they were willing and desirous to learn; to the multitude who would not learn, who cared for nothing but the outward kingdom, he left them unexplained. This is indeed the reason for using parables which he himself assigned in his reply to the disciples.

On the present occasion he delivered the fine and instructive parable of the Sower, — a very suitable one to form the beginning of this mode of teaching; for it described, in a striking manner, the different characters of those by whom his doctrine had been hitherto heard, and the various effects it had had on various dispositions. To many he had preached in vain, for their minds were preoccupied with prejudices, pleasures, or cares. Some had been affected for a time, but had taken offence and deserted him. Some had been decoyed away by a too great love of the world, and some by fear of unpopularity and persecution. Some had remained faithful and steadfast. All these characters are exhibited in the parable; and we may suppose that it was this observation of the manner in which his own preaching had been received that led him to choose for his first lesson, on changing his mode of instruction, a subject so striking in itself, and so applicable as well as useful to all times and communities.

He then recited several parables illustrative of the character and progress of his kingdom. The first was that of the tares of the field, which he afterward expounded in private to his disciples. The others related to the growth and extension of his doctrine, and strikingly manifest the confidence which he felt in its final prevalence and triumph. After returning home, he added several others for the instruction of his immediate followers, designed to express the value of the object to which they had devoted themselves, and to teach the certainty of a future retribution.

After this, Jesus left Capernaum, and made another visit to his own town of Nazareth. It was about five months since he had there been assaulted and expelled by the citizens. It was now to be seen whether the increase of his reputation through the land might not have prepared their minds to receive him more favorably. But their prejudices had not been removed. They could not forget that he was one of themselves, and they would not believe that their humble townsman could be a prophet. "Is not this the carpenter?" said they. "Are not his brothers and sisters with us?" A few only brought their sick to him; and thus, because of their obstinate unbelief, at which he is said to have wondered, he could do but few miracles there. Thus he proved the truth of his own saying, A prophet is everywhere honored, except in his own country.

Matthew xiii. 53. Mark vi. i.

CHAPTER XIII.

DEATH OF JOHN THE BAPTIST. — JESUS FEEDS THE MULTITUDES. — RETURNS TO CAPERNAUM. — CONVERSES IN THE SYNAGOGUE.

About this time took place the death of John the Baptist. Herodias, wife of Herod, at whose instigation he had been imprisoned, would willingly have put him to death in the beginning; but Herod, who had a great respect for him, and moreover knew how the people honored him, would consent to do no more than imprison him.

Herodias was resolved to accomplish her purpose at the first convenient opportunity. Such an one presented itself on the birthday of Herod, when he gave a great entertainment to his lords, and high captains, and the chief estates of Galilee. She then sent in her daughter, Salome, to dance before the king and his guests. This was a great condescension on the part of this young lady, because public dancing was not considered becoming in persons of rank. Hence it was the greater compliment to the occasion; and Herod, in the

Matthew xiv. i. Mark vi. 14. Luke ix. 7.

excitement of the moment, took an oath that he would grant her any favor that she should ask. She consulted her mother; and that cunning and revengeful woman bade her ask the head of John the Baptist. Herod perceived the snare in which he had been taken, and would gladly have retracted. But he had bound himself by an oath, and was urged on by those who sat with him at table, and he therefore commanded it to be done. John was beheaded in prison, and his head given to Salome, who carried it to her infamous mother. The crime did not go unpunished. In the first place, Herod was defeated in battle by Aretas, king of Arabia, whose daughter he had set aside in order to marry Herodias. Josephus declares that all the people regarded this as a judgment from heaven for his treatment of John. Afterwards, Herodias, being ambitious that her husband should enjoy as high a title as her brother Agrippa, the king, persuaded him to go to Rome and seek it of the Emperor. But the Emperor, having reason to doubt his loyalty, instead of advancing him to dignity, banished him to Lyons, and then to Spain. Such was the punishment which Providence brought upon the complicated wickedness of this petty prince.

Herod appears to have been haunted and made miserable by the consciousness of his guilt. We read that when he heard the reports of the wonderful works of Jesus, he thought it must be John risen from the dead; and though his courtiers endeavored to persuade him that it was rather Elias, or some other of the ancient prophets, his disturbed fancy still represented him as the man whom he had so unjustly destroyed.

It seems at first view strange that Herod should now hear of Jesus for the first time, when he had been for so long a period active in the province. Tiberias, the seat of government, was not far from Capernaum; and although it does not appear that Jesus had visited that city, yet it is evident that the reports concerning him must have reached it. It is probable, therefore, that during our Lord's ministry thus far Herod had been absent from Galilee. It has been supposed by some that this was the season of his war with Aretas; that it was his soldiers, marching toward Arabia, who some months before had inquired their duty of John the Baptist; and that it was immediately on his return from that war, that he made his birthday feast, and put the Baptist to death. If so, then he had been absent from Galilee during the whole of our Lord's ministry thus far; and this explains why he has never been mentioned in the course of the history, and why the fame of Jesus was new to him. Others suppose that this must have been the year when he made a journey to Rome. In either case the difficulty is removed. But if we should suppose that Jesus had been preaching in Galilee two or three years, instead of a few months, the difficulty would be insuperable.

When Jesus heard of the death of John, he immediately retired across the lake with his apostles. Herod had expressed a desire to see him; but he did not choose to put himself in the power of that cunning man, and therefore from this time forward spent very little time in Galilee, or indeed in any one place. He now retreated to a desert spot in the neighborhood of Bethsaida, in the dominions of Philip. The people soon discovered whither he had gone, and went by land to the same place "from all the cities." It was impossible to avoid them, and he went upon a hill and taught them, and healed their sick.

When the day drew toward a close, the disciples suggested that the multitudes must be wearied and faint, and that it would be well to send them away to the villages for refreshment. But Jesus chose the opportunity for a new display of his power, such as had not yet been made, and such as was likely to appeal to the minds of many who had been little affected by his other works. It is well worthy of observation, how he varied the character of his miracles, that he might suit them to every variety of disposition, and give to all ca-

Matthew xiv. 13. Mark vi. 35. Luke ix. 10. John vi. 1.

pacities the opportunity to be convinced. On the present occasion, he resolved to feed the multitude himself, instead of sending them away. He accordingly directed his disciples to arrange them in companies of fifty persons, and make them sit down on the grass. It was thus ascertained that the number of people was about five thousand; which gives us some idea of the magnitude of the crowds which usually attended our Lord. It is possible that his being in a new place may have called together many who had no previous opportunity of seeing the celebrated prophet; but otherwise there is no reason to suppose that this was a larger number than frequently assembled round him.

However this may be, their astonishment and admiration may well have been extreme, when they found that they were thus seated on the hillside for the purpose of being fed by two fishes and five loaves of bread; when they saw this scanty pittance multiply as it passed through their ranks; and, after their hunger was fully satisfied, saw the apostles gather up twelve baskets full of the uneaten remnants. This new and signal wonder excited them to a high pitch of enthusiasm. They were now sure that this was the Messiah. They were sure there could be no risk in proclaiming him such, for he would be able to support any number of followers at his pleasure.

Perhaps they even fancied that he designed in this act to intimate his readiness to provide for those who would adhere to him. At any rate, they thought that now the hour was come, the long-desired hour. With one voice they declared he should be King, and were ready to use violence to compel him. When Jesus perceived this, he immediately *constrained* his disciples, as Mark expresses it (thereby intimating that they were disposed to join the multitude), to get into the boat, and commanded them to go to Bethsaida; — not the town in whose neighborhood they were, but another village "on the other side," just south of Capernaum, called Bethsaida in Galilee. He himself remained behind, and persuaded the multitude to disperse. Then, it being one of the extraordinary and trying moments of his life, he returned to the mountain and prayed.

Meanwhile the night came on, and the disciples, in their little boat, being detained by a contrary wind, had not reached the place they had designed. The whole night was passed in a vain attempt to resist the wind. At the fourth watch, that is, about three o'clock in the morning, as they were still toiling at the oars, Jesus, who had seen their distress from the land, approached them, walking on the water. At first they thought it an apparition, and cried out for fear. But his well-known voice reached them, saying, "It is I, be not afraid." The ardent Peter, delighted to behold his Master and eager to embrace him, asked leave to go to him on the waves. Jesus said, "Come." But when Peter found himself actually on the water, his courage failed, and he would have sunk if his Master had not stretched forth his hand and caught him. "O thou of little faith," said he, "wherefore didst thou doubt?" When they arrived on board, the wind ceased, and they easily reached their haven.

They went ashore in the land of Gennesaret, which was the name of a considerable tract of fertile, populous country bordering the west side of the lake. The tidings of his arrival spread rapidly among the people, and it seemed as if they could not do enough to testify their joy. They sent out into all the country round about, and brought to him in beds those that were diseased. And wherever he moved, whether to cities, or villages, or the country, his way was thronged with objects on which to exert his benevolent power. They laid the sick in the streets, and, remembering the woman who had been healed in the streets of Capernaum, besought him that they might touch if it were only the hem of his garment; and as many as touched him were made whole. There is no more lively description of the sensation his appearance created and of the

Matthew xiv. 34. Mark vi. 54.

wonderful works he did, than is found in this account of his visit to Gennesaret. In this manner he proceeded through the country till he reached Capernaum.

Here he was met by some persons whom he had left the preceding day on the opposite side of the water. They had been surprised not to find him in the morning; for they had seen the disciples go away without him, and there was no other boat at the place; — they could not conjecture how he could have departed. But, not finding him, they went on board some vessels just arrived from Tiberias, and sailed over to Capernaum to inquire for him. They found him, to their no small amazement, in the synagogue. He received them coldly; he told them, that it was not in a right spirit that they sought him, but merely because they had seen the miracle of the loaves, and therefore trusted that he would support his followers. He endeavored to lead them away from their wrong notions respecting the Messiah. Some of them asked of him a sufficient proof that he was he, pretending that his miracle of the preceding day was nothing in comparison with that of the manna given by Moses. Others seemed more docile, and begged him to give them the true bread of which he spoke. But, on the whole, they manifested so unteachable, prejudiced, and

John vi. 22.

worldly a state of mind, they so carped and cavilled at his expressions, that he did as he had before done, clothed his ideas in strong figures. These they chose to interpret literally, and took great offence at them. Insomuch that many who had been accounted his disciples, being now satisfied that his character and purposes were wholly different from what they had hoped, that he would not be their king and was very rigid in his religious requisitions, deserted him and went away. Their desertion evidently affected him; and he turned to the twelve with something like strong feeling, and said, "Will ye also go away?" But they knew him too intimately to leave him. Though they did not fully comprehend, they deeply reverenced and loved him, and entirely believed in him. Peter answered for them all, without hesitation, "Lord, to whom should we go? thou hast the words of eternal life; and we believe and are sure that thou art the Holy One of God." Doubtless this ready and hearty reply was soothing to his Master's wounded feelings. But still there was sadness in the thought that even of these twelve all were not to be trusted. True, said he, you believe in me; I have chosen you; and yet one even of you will be false to me; — "One of you is a devil," a false accuser, a traitor.

CHAPTER XIV.

JESUS MAKES EXCURSIONS TO TYRE AND SIDON.— TO DALMANUTHA. — TO CESAREA PHILIPPI. — HE SPEAKS OF HIS DEATH.

The desire, already mentioned, to avoid the snares of Herod, who had now returned to his province, and whose capital was not far distant from Capernaum, appears to have been the reason why Jesus, immediately after the conversations just related, left his own town again, and made a distant excursion, in a northerly direction, to the borders of Tyre and Sidon. These were places of great celebrity, lying on the shore of the Mediterranean Sea, near the extreme corner of Palestine. They had been assigned, in the original distribution of the country, to the tribe of Ashur; but as the ancient inhabitants were never dispossessed, they did not properly become Jewish cities. It was not therefore for the purpose of preaching the Gospel that our Lord went thither, for his ministry was confined to the Jews. It must have been for some such cause as that which has just been mentioned.

Matthew xv. 21. Mark vii. 24.

For the same reason it was, that, as Mark tells us, he desired that no one might know he was there. However, it was not possible that he should be concealed; and a woman, whose daughter was suffering in a peculiarly distressful manner, learning that he was there, made her way to him, and earnestly entreated his compassionate aid. He at first refused, because she was a Gentile, and he was sent to the Jews only. When she still insisted, and would not be denied, he refused her yet more strongly, saying that his bread was for the children, and he could not give it to dogs, — a term by which we may suppose the Jews were accustomed to designate the Gentiles. Even this reply, harsh as it seemed, did not discourage the persevering mother. It was not intended to do so, but to draw forth and display her faith. This it effected; and she made that respectful and beautiful answer, which has always been admired, and which won our Saviour's admiration. True, Lord, said she; the bread is for the children; but the dogs may have the crumbs which fall from the table. Jesus immediately answered, "For this saying, go thy way; great is thy faith." And, for the reward of her faith, she found her daughter healed.

No other incident during this excursion is recorded, nor are we informed how long a period was consumed in it. And we have no ground on which to build a conjecture.

Returning from the neighborhood of Tyre and Sidon, he passed through parts of Decapolis, still out of the jurisdiction of Herod, and came to the sea of Galilee. Here again crowds collected about him, and he did many miracles among them; one of which, the cure of a person deaf and dumb, is particularly recorded by Mark. After being with them three days, he took compassion on them, as it was an uninhabited place, and did for them as he had, under similar circumstances, done for the people in the vicinity of Bethsaida, — he distributed among them the little food which his disciples had with them, and, by miraculously multiplying it, satisfied the hunger of more than four thousand persons. He then dismissed them; and, taking ship, sailed to Dalmanutha and Magdala. These places, of which nothing very material is known, were situated toward the southern extremity of the lake, on the eastern side, nearly opposite to Tiberias. Here those perpetual cavillers, the Pharisees, assailed him, asking him for a sign from heaven. This was their old refuge, — to pretend that they would believe on him, if they could but see a sign from heaven, while yet they were disbelieving and disparaging all the wonderful things he was

Matthew xv. 29, xvi. 1. Mark vii. 31, viii. 1.

daily doing. What would such men believe? Evidently nothing; and therefore, aware of their unfairness and weary with their hypocritical importunities, Jesus refused to gratify them; told them that any man with his eyes open might discern the signs of the times; and that no sign should be given to so evil a generation, but that of the prophet Jonah.

Leaving this place, he again took ship for the purpose of crossing the lake. While on the passage, he alluded to what had just passed, and bade his disciples beware of the leaven of the Pharisees and Sadducees. And here he was obliged to observe, as was often the case, how slow even his devoted friends were to comprehend his meaning. Much as they were accustomed to his mode of speaking, they yet stupidly supposed, that, in this remark, he meant to blame them for forgetting to put bread on board the boat. He was obliged to explain to them, that he meant the doctrine, and not the bread, of the Pharisees. This is a little thing perhaps; but we may easily see how his spirit must have been sometimes tried and his hopes damped by dulness and want of faith in those whom he taught. It must have been no small trial, when about to commit his religion to the care of these men, to find that they did not comprehend it, and to be obliged to complain of them as of "little faith," "slow of heart to understand."

They landed at Bethsaida, on the upper end of the lake. Here he restored sight to a blind man, in a very private way, as if he desired to avoid notice, and then proceeded with his disciples to Cesarea Philippi. This city was about forty miles directly north of Bethsaida. It stood near to the ancient Laish, or possibly on the same site. It had been rebuilt by Philip, the present tetrarch of the province, and was named by him Cesarea, in honor of the Emperor. His own name was added, in order to distinguish it from another Cesarea on the coast. It was a place of some note. What was the object of our Lord's visit there is not stated. As far as can be judged from circumstances, he was simply seeking to avoid Herod, until the time when he should go up to Jerusalem. Hence his journey was private, without crowds, miracles, or discourses; — at least none are recorded.

One circumstance, however, is related, which serves to show the state of his mind, and formed the beginning of a new era in his history. He knew that his ministry was soon to end, and that he must leave his great plans to be carried on by the few affectionate men that were with him. He knew that they were devoted to him with zealous hearts, yet he had seen something of their dulness, and was aware that they did not fully un-

Mark viii. 22.

derstand him. Would they have strength to bear the disappointment of their hopes, and adhere to him faithfully, when they should find that the loss of all earthly honors awaited them? As yet he had not spoken to them directly on this subject. He had not revealed to them, that he was to be taken from them by a violent and disgraceful death. It was necessary to break to them the truth.

The present seemed to be the suitable time for doing it. He was at a distance from the ordinary sphere of his labors, and the scene of his recent triumphs. Instead of being accompanied by thousands of grateful and admiring men, who hung on his lips, rejoiced in his benevolent power, and longed to proclaim him king, he was hurrying privately from place to place, attended only by a few tried friends, seeking concealment from the tyrant who had just put his harbinger to death. All this must have perplexed his disciples. How is it, they would say, that just as all seemed ripe for the explosion, instead of availing himself of the advantageous crisis, he shuns it; avoids the people, seeks retirement, does few miracles, and those almost by stealth? Jesus felt that such thoughts must be passing through the minds of his followers, and must severely perplex them. What wonder if they should even waver in their

Matthew xvi. 13. Mark viii. 27. Luke ix. 18.

opinion, and doubt whether, after all, he were the Messiah? He might be only a forerunner, as many men supposed him.

In order therefore to ascertain the state of their minds, and prepare the way for the yet more fearful disclosures that must soon be made, he speaks to them on the subject. He asks them, first, what is the general opinion of men respecting himself. They tell him that opinions are various. Some think him to be John the Baptist, some Elijah, and others say that one of the old prophets is risen again. That is, his course had been so different from what they anticipated in the Messiah, that men generally did not believe him to be he, though they were willing to think him a great prophet sent to prepare the way. Jesus then asked their own opinion; had they also been so disappointed at this change in his affairs as to doubt respecting him? "Whom say ye that I am?" Peter immediately replied, "Thou art the Christ." There was no hesitation. The answer was direct, frank, hearty. It proved that nothing had occurred to shake their confidence, or cause a serious doubt. Jesus rewarded the heartiness of the confession by a strong expression of pleasure and approbation. "Blessed art thou, Simon, son of Jonas," he exclaimed; "for flesh and blood hath not revealed this unto thee, but my Father who is in heaven." And then added that distinguished promise, "I say unto thee, thou art Peter," — a rock indeed, — "and on this rock I will build my church; and the gates of hell shall not prevail against it."

Thus it was evident that the minds of the twelve did not waver; and this emphatic promise to Peter was eminently adapted to encourage and confirm them. But there was more yet to be done. He had now at length, for the first time as it would seem, solemnly and formally recognized the title of Messiah, in the presence of his followers. They might think themselves at liberty immediately to act upon it, and proclaim him to the people. But this would be inconsistent with the designs of Providence. He therefore strictly forbade it. "He charged them straitly, that they should tell no man of him." He would not have them publish his titles and office until they rightly understood them; and he went on to explain to them that they did not rightly understand them. He told them that, instead of a triumphant, he was to be a suffering leader; instead of an army and a throne, the homage of the people and the dominion of the nations, he must go to Jerusalem, "and suffer many things from the elders, chief priests, and scribes, and be put to death, and rise again the third day."

They heard these words with dismay. How contrary to their expectations, how opposed to all their notions of their Messiah's fortunes! Peter, with his usual ardor and boldness, loudly expressed his feelings. He expostulated with his Master, insisted that it must not, and should not, be as he had said. He not improbably went further, and attempted to persuade him to resist forcibly the oppression of which he had spoken. Jesus, whose meekness and gentleness formed a strong contrast to the vehemence of his disciple, was hurt at this violent outbreak of zeal, and saw the necessity of checking it at once; it might easily lead to most disastrous consequences. Therefore "he turned and looked on his disciples," says Mark, that they might observe how positive and resolved he was, and loudly rebuked Peter as influenced by a worldly ambition and a regard to human honors, rather than by a religious regard to the will and purposes of God. Then turning to all his disciples, in the hearing of the people, he with great solemnity urged on them the duty of adhering to their profession at every risk, and through all hardships of self-denial. If they would have the advantages and glories of his kingdom, they must be ready to relinquish their selfish hopes, to take up the cross, and even surrender their lives. They were pledged to a suffering and despised Master, they must not be ashamed of him, they must acknowledge him before man; otherwise, he would not acknowledge and honor them in the great day of his real glory. For, he assured them, he should come in the glory of his Father and of the angels, and bring to every one a reward according to his character and fidelity. Thus he encouraged them by the solemn and magnificent promise of a final triumph, notwithstanding what he had just taught them of his approaching sufferings and disgrace. And that this might the more forcibly impress them, he ended with saying, that there were some present among them who should not taste of death till they had seen the kingdom of God coming with power. Thus mingling the new vision of evil he had just opened to them with a stern precept of duty and an animating prospect of glory, he sought to make on them that profound impression which would prepare them to meet with firmness and constancy the trials before them.

The lesson was not lost on them. Oftentimes, doubtless, in after days, when they were preaching the doctrines of their despised master in the midst of obloquy and scorn, of peril, privation, and death, they recalled to mind the powerful words in which he had first taught them, that they must endure suffering for his sake, and follow in the bloody path of his cross to their reward; and when they did so, and then remembered how he had suffered and was now glorified, they felt themselves armed to endure all things for his sake; they braved persecution and torture; they confessed him before men in prison and amid flames, and died rejoicing in the confidence that he would confess them before his Father in heaven.

It is not they only to whom those precepts respecting self-denial and the necessity of owning our holy Master were addressed. To none are they inapplicable, who hope to enter on the future life which he has revealed.

CHAPTER XV.

THE TRANSFIGURATION. — JESUS RETURNS TO CAPERNAUM. — PASSES THROUGH PERÆA TOWARD JERUSALEM.

WHILE the minds of the disciples were in a state of amazement at the new prospect opened before them, an event took place calculated to enlighten and instruct them, as well as to prepare them for their coming trials. Six days after the scene recorded at the close of the last chapter, Jesus took his three confidential apostles, Peter, James, and John, and retired with them to a mountain for purposes of devotion; — another example of his custom to devote a season to special prayer at every important crisis of his life. While he prayed, his appearance became changed, his countenance shone with a lustre like that of the sun, and his raiment was white as the light. At the same time Moses and Elijah, the two great names of the ancient dispensation, appeared to him, and conversed with him respecting his approaching death at Jerusalem. Perhaps they

Matthew xvii. 1. Mark ix. 2. Luke ix. 28.

were sent to reveal to him fully all its purposes and necessity. Perhaps, as, when he afterward prayed earnestly in the garden, an angel was sent to strengthen him, so now, as he prayed on the mountain, these holy prophets were sent to cheer him and help him to meet his fearful trials. This however we do not know, and there is no room to enter into a discussion of all the questions to which this remarkable event has given rise. One thing is clear. It was designed to give a Divine testimony to the character and authority of Jesus; for, as the prophets departed and the bright cloud moved away, a voice was heard saying, "This is my beloved Son; hear him." Peter afterwards, in one of his Epistles, refers to this voice "from the excellent glory" as one of the evidences of his Master's truth. As they went down from the mountain, Jesus forbade the three witnesses to speak of it until he had risen from the dead. Mark tells us that they observed the injunction, but were greatly perplexed to understand what was meant by the rising from the dead. None of the apostles seem to have arrived at any right apprehension on this subject during their Lord's life; and we shall find, as we go on, that his various attempts to explain it were lost upon them. There is reason to suppose that they thought it, not a recovery from actual death, — for it was a current opinion among the Jews that the Messiah should never die, — but a rising to the power and office of his kingdom.

But if they could not understand what was meant by the resurrection, neither could they comprehend why they should conceal what they had seen. There was a tradition, derived from the prophet Malachi, that Elijah should appear before the coming of the Messiah. Why should they not proclaim that they had seen him on the mountain? They asked an explanation; and Jesus informed them that Elijah had already appeared, and been put to death. The office described by Malachi had been performed by John the Baptist.

On reaching the plain, they found the other disciples surrounded by a crowd, and among them a man with a lunatic son, whom the disciples had in vain striven to heal. Jesus reproved them for their want of faith, and healed the unfortunate boy. When questioned by the apostles why they had not been able to do it, he answered, "Because of your unbelief"; and assured them that if their faith were but strong, no miracle would be impossible to them. And their faith was to be rendered thus strong, he added, by prayer and fasting, — by faithful use of the means of devotion and spiritual strength.

It has been thought that the beautiful and pic-

Matthew xvii. 14. Mark ix. 14. Luke ix. 37.

turesque mountain of Tabor was that on which the transfiguration took place. But the summit of Tabor was far too public a spot for a transaction of this nature; and besides, the course of the history shows that it could not have occurred in Galilee, and that it probably took place in the neighborhood of Cesarea Philippi.

Shortly after this event, they directed their way to Galilee, and returned to Capernaum, from which they had been for some time absent. Their return was private, for Jesus was desirous of concealing his movements as far as possible; "he would not that any one should know it." Perhaps he would not have returned home at all, except that it might be necessary for some purposes previous to his final departure for Jerusalem. As they journeyed, the subject of his approaching end appears to have occupied their minds; indeed how could it be otherwise? "Let these sayings sink deep into your ears," said he; "the Son of man shall be delivered into the hands of men, and they will kill him. But he will rise again the third day." But they understood not this saying, says the Evangelist, and were afraid to ask him. Hence it remained without explanation, and they put upon it that construction which was most consonant to their prejudices and wishes,—a construction which afterwards entirely misled them.

On arriving at Capernaum, the officers whose

duty it was to collect a certain tax inquired of Peter whether his Master did not pay it. Peter, aware that Jesus had resided long enough in Capernaum to have it considered his lawful home, replied that he did. It is not perfectly clear what this tax was. It was perhaps the poll-tax levied by the Romans; but more probably it was the tax of half a shekel required to be paid by all Jews of twenty years old and upward for the use of the temple. When Peter went into the house to speak of the subject to Jesus, his Lord immediately explained to him that, as the princes of the earth do not assess their own children, he, as the Son of God, would be rightfully excused from the payment of a tax to the temple, which was his Father's house. He probably said this because he desired at this critical period to impress on his followers, by every possible means, the assurance of his authority and dignity. For now the season was coming in which their steadfastness would be tried. Yet, that he might give no unnecessary offence, he paid the tax; and, what is very remarkable, by performing a miracle, — the only instance in which he wrought a miracle for his own convenience.

Immediately after this an incident occurred which shows the extreme difficulty in which he was placed in relation to the disciples. If he

Matthew xvii. 24.

spoke of his sufferings and death, they were in sorrow and despair. If to cheer them he spoke of his resurrection, or asserted his dignity, as he had just done when speaking of the tax, they immediately misunderstood him, and indulged erroneous expectations. Such, it now appeared, had been the result of his recent communications. They contrived to satisfy themselves, that, whatever their Lord might mean, he could not mean to give up the kingdom of Israel and the throne of David; and as the time seemed to be drawing nigh, they began to be desirous of knowing what offices they should possess and what privileges enjoy. This had been a topic of speculation with them on their journey from Cesarea Philippi, and was carried so far as to occasion some dispute. They could not agree which of them ought to hold the highest offices, or be "the greatest," as they expressed it. Now nothing could be less agreeable to the mind of their Master than such a strife as this. It showed not only a spirit of ambition and rivalry, but a desire of worldly distinction. Jesus, therefore, took an early opportunity to rebuke it; and he did it in that impressive way which was so characteristic of him. He called the twelve together to him in the house, and placed a little child before them. There, said he, is your example. Unless you give up this

Matthew xviii. Mark ix. 33. Luke ix. 46.

ambitious desire of personal distinction, and humble yourselves like children, instead of attaining high places in my kingdom, you will not even have any place in it. If any of you insist on being first, he shall be last of all and servant of all. And thus he went on, warning them against ambition, urging them to severe and self-denying virtue, and to mutual kindness, forbearance, and forgiveness, in a discourse at once the most solemn and affectionate. They could not have heard it without strong emotion. It seems as if it must have removed from their hearts forever all ambitious rivalry and unkind feeling. For he illustrated it by parables, setting forth the infinite grace and long-suffering of God in representations so wonderfully affecting, that all selfish pride and unrelenting hardness of disposition are made to seem despicable.

With this conversation our Lord closed his ministry in Galilee. It began, as we may judge from the first public discourse upon record, with benedictions on the meek, the humble, the forgiving, as if he thus would paint the character and display the genius of his religion. And we have just seen that it closed with pathetically impressing on his chosen twelve the same great lessons, — lessons difficult to be learned, but which form the loveliness of the Christian character.

And now, says the Evangelist, "when the time was come that he should be received up, he steadfastly set his face to go to Jerusalem." He knew what awaited him, but he would not shrink from it. The great work for which he had been sent into the world, and which he had devoted himself to accomplish, could not be complete except through his death. And he went steadfastly forward to meet it. He went, in one sense, alone. His nearest friends did not comprehend his situation. From them, therefore, he had no true sympathy. If he talked with them, they misunderstood his words. None but God knew what was before him; with none but God could he commune on the dreadful and mysterious fate which was approaching. But he felt that he heard him always; and he was not alone, for his Father was with him.

On leaving Capernaum, he at first attempted to pass by the direct route to Judæa, which lies through Samaria. But he was refused admittance into one of the towns, because he was going up to the great feast at Jerusalem. Such was the religious bigotry of that people against the Jews. The disciples, who not only had a strong attachment to their Lord, but who were expecting him soon to appear in his glory as the Messiah, were highly indignant at so insulting treatment;

Matthew xix. 1. Mark x. 1. Luke ix. 51.

and James and John carried the feeling so far, that they proposed to him to call down fire from heaven upon them, as Elijah had once done. But Jesus had no sympathy with such feelings or measures. He turned and rebuked them, saying, "Ye know not what manner of spirit ye are of." And then, to avoid all contention, he gave up his original plan, crossed the Jordan, and proceeded on his way through the country which lies on the other side of the river.

His journey thus lay through Peræa, a region which he had once or twice before visited, but where probably he was in general known only by reputation. The people resorted to him as he passed, and he taught and healed them. He was still in Herod's dominions; but his reasons for privacy seem to have existed no longer, now that he was secure of reaching Jerusalem in season for the feast. He went publicly, in company doubtless with the people who at this time must have been thronging the roads on the way to the city. He was one day warned by some Pharisees, that Herod was in pursuit of him, and advised to flee: "Get thee out, and depart hence; for Herod will kill thee." But he replied, that he feared him not; that he should proceed on his way, teaching and working miracles, for two days; and on the third should finish his errand and be out of the reach of the crafty prince. No one could now hinder him from completing his work; for it was not possible for a prophet to perish out of Jerusalem. And when he had said this, being deeply affected at the thought of the guilt and the wretchedness of that devoted city, he burst out in the pathetic exclamation: "O Jerusalem, Jerusalem, thou that killest the prophets and stonest them that are sent unto thee, how often would I have gathered thy children together, as a hen gathereth her brood under her wings! and ye would not. Behold, your house is left unto you desolate."

This last journey to Jerusalem was signalized by many incidents and discourses. It was at this time that the Pharisees came to him, and attempted to ensnare him by subtile questions about the law of marriage and divorce; whom he silenced by the clearness and wisdom of his replies. Now it was, too, that certain parents brought to him their little children, that they might share the attention and receive the blessing of the benevolent teacher. The disciples did not understand how suitable this was to their Master's character, and they rebuked those who brought them. But Jesus, who had so lately recommended the example of a child to his ambitious followers, was pleased to show his affection and honor for the little innocents. He therefore encouraged the

Luke xiii. 31. Matthew xix. 3.

parents whom the apostles had refused, and took their children to his arms and blessed them; saying, "Suffer the children to come to me, and forbid them not; for of such is the kingdom of God." He then reminded his mistaken friends of what he had so recently taught them, — that it was only by being like these children that they could enter into his kingdom, or be partakers of the real blessings he had come to dispense.

It was during this journey also, that a rich young man came to him, earnestly inquiring what he should do to inherit eternal life. There was something so prepossessing in his appearance of amiableness and sincerity, that Jesus is said to have looked on him with peculiar complacency. But amiable dispositions, and sincerity of purpose, are of themselves insufficient; and he required him to give proof of his attachment to principle and to himself, by distributing his property in charity, and devoting himself to his ministry. This was more than the ardent young man could bring himself to do; and he departed, "sorrowing," it is said; for he would have been glad to attach himself to the Messiah, if he could have done it without a sacrifice. His riches were the obstacle; and our Lord took occasion to remark how dangerous a possession is wealth, and how likely to deter men from the reception of his Gos-

Matthew xix. 13. Mark x. 13. Luke xviii. 15.

pel. They would be slow to give up for its sake their worldly enjoyments and luxuries.

On hearing this, Peter reminded his Master that he and his companions had given up everything for the sake of following him, and asked what reward they were to have. Jesus answered him in terms adapted to encourage and satisfy him in the highest degree. He assured him that those who suffered loss and sacrifice for him and his Gospel should receive abundant recompense even in this world, — meaning, doubtless, in those solid satisfactions and pleasures which attend the performance of duty, — and in the world to come everlasting life. In this connection he recited the parable of the laborers in the vineyard; and about the same time, probably, delivered some other of his recorded instructions.

Thus they proceeded towards Jerusalem; and "as they were in the way," says the Evangelist, "Jesus went before them; and they were amazed, and as they followed they were sore afraid." These words express the perplexity and apprehension of mind with which they looked forward to the result of their journey. He again spoke to them on the subject, endeavoring to explain to them what it was that was to happen. But they still understood none of these things. So far indeed were they from any just idea of what he meant, that James and John, at this very time, came to him with their mother, to obtain from him a promise that they should have the first offices of honor in his kingdom; that they should sit, the one at his right hand, and the other at his left. Whether this request originated with these disciples, or was wholly the suggestion of their mother, who was certainly very forward in it, does not appear. It is in either case wonderful that, so soon after the rebuke which had been given to their ambitious projects, they should have been so infatuated as to present this demand. The other ten were not a little displeased; and their Master took the opportunity to reprove once more, and in the plainest terms, this love of superiority and power; declaring, that, however it might be among the leading men of the world, greatness among his followers was to be attained only by services and toils; "even as the Son of man," he added, "came not to be ministered unto, but to minister, and to give his life a ransom for many."

At length having arrived at the point in the road where it crosses the Jordan, in order to go to Jerusalem, he passed over. Jericho lies on the road from the river, and must be traversed. This was an ancient and populous city, celebrated as the first place taken by Joshua, when the armies of Israel entered Canaan. It was situated in a

Matthew xx. 17. Mark x. 32. Luke xviii. 31.

spacious plain, abounding in palm-trees, and was often styled the City of Palms. In the time of our Saviour it was a place of considerable wealth and splendor, having been adorned by Herod with a palace and other public buildings, in the magnificent spirit of that prince. As our Lord, with his numerous attendants, approached this busy and populous town, the rumor of his coming went before him, and the citizens poured out from the gates to meet him, — eager to behold the venerable prophet of whom report had told such wonders. One or two blind men, hearing the noise of the multitude passing, asked what it meant; and being answered that it was Jesus of Nazareth, they called out to him in earnest and confident faith, as the son of David, that is, the Messiah, to have pity on them. Jesus did not refuse the title, and restored them to sight, to the great admiration of the crowds who witnessed the miracle.

Amongst those whom the fame of his coming had brought out to the highway was Zacchæus, chief of the publicans, a man of distinction and property. In his eagerness to catch a sight of the distinguished stranger, he climbed into a sycamore-tree by the way-side, and waited his arrival at the spot. Jesus drew nigh; and, to the great amazement of Zacchæus, — who could not hope that so despised a person as an unpopular publican would

Luke xix. 1.

be thought worthy the notice of a great prophet, — looked up into the tree, and bade him hasten down, for he intended to honor his house with his presence. Thus did our Lord delight to show regard to the unpretending; thus did he often verify his words, that they who humble themselves shall be exalted.

As might have been expected, this distinction given a man of odious profession, "a sinner" as he was styled, gave offence to the people, and they did not hesitate to express their displeasure. But Zacchæus defended himself against the imputations they would cast on his character, and Jesus boldly vindicated the cause he had taken. He told the murmurers, that, though they might regard this man as a sinner, he looked upon him as a son of Abraham; he approved the dispositions he had manifested; he proclaimed salvation to his house; for, in truth, he added in the words of his favorite expression, he had come to seek and to save those that were lost, — not to join in depressing and condemning them.

Jesus passed the day at the house of Zacchæus. There was an evident expectation in the company assembled with him there that he was about to assume the kingdom, and they thought his approach to Jerusalem a sign of it. This led him to recite the parable of the ten pounds; in which he represented to them the true character of his kingdom, taught them how solemn would be the responsibility of those who should enter it, instructed them in the use they should make of their opportunities and advantages, and admonished them of the fearful account to be rendered by the unfaithful.

He then left Jericho, and proceeded toward Jerusalem, distant about twenty miles. On the sixth day before the Passover he reached Bethany. As this was only two miles from Jerusalem, a large part of the concourse of people who attended him probably went forward to the city, and spread the report of his approach. Many of the Jews, on hearing it, went out to see him,—not only on his own account, but for the sake of seeing at the same time Lazarus, whom he had raised from the grave. The chief priests, who had already adopted measures for the apprehension of Jesus, took it seriously into consideration whether Lazarus also should not be put to death; because, as long as he should live, he would be the means of inducing many to believe in him who had restored him to life.

John xii. 1.

CHAPTER XVI.

JESUS ENTERS JERUSALEM IN TRIUMPH. — EVENTS OF THE FIRST DAY. — THE GREEKS DESIRE TO SEE HIM. — HE RETIRES TO BETHANY.

ALTHOUGH it was yet six days before the Passover, the people had already collected in great numbers at Jerusalem. There were certain legal defilements which required purification, some of them for seven days, before the feast could be partaken. This obliged many to resort early to the city; and it is reasonable to suppose that, in many instances, they were accompanied by their friends. Hence it is easy to see that the crowd must have been gathering for several days; and St. John informs us, that, as they met and talked in the courts of the temple, there was a general inquiry for Jesus. "What think ye?" said they, "will he not come to the feast?" They remembered how he had been treated at his former visits to the city; how he had been harassed and stoned; and how but four months ago, at the feast of Dedication, he had been obliged to fly for his life, be-

John xi. 55.

fore he had been there a day. They knew, too, that there was a proclamation abroad against him, and that the chief council had given commandment, that, if any man knew where he was, he should inform of it, that he might be seized. It was therefore a great matter of inquiry among the people, whether he would venture, at this obvious risk of his life, to show himself at the feast. They did not know, as he did, that his time was come, and he would shun danger no longer.

It must have been with no little surprise that they heard, on Saturday evening, the report of his arrival at Bethany. On former occasions he had come late and privately. But now he was among the first to arrive, and was coming publicly. The strong sentiment of grateful admiration prevailed; and, in spite of the decrees of the ruling powers, there was a spontaneous movement in the multitude to do honor to the benevolent prophet. The next morning, therefore, they went out to meet him, and conduct him into the city. All history does not record a more genuine instance of enthusiastic public homage. It was the more striking in this case because so transient.

Meantime Jesus had left Bethany; and as he went toward Jerusalem he sent two of his disciples into the village of Bethphage, which lay just

Matthew xxi. 1. Mark xi. 1. Luke xix. 29. John xii. 12.

off the highway, with directions to bring to him a young ass, which they should find tied with its dam at the entrance of the village. It undoubtedly belonged to one of his friends and followers, as the owner at once allowed it to be taken, on being told, "the Lord hath need of him." Some of the disciples placed their garments on the beast, and Jesus sat upon him. This seemed to the attending multitude a signal that he was now to assume the rank and title which they believed to be his, and they set no limits to their expressions of delight and transport. They took off their garments, and laid them in the path; they cut down branches from the trees, and strewed them in the way. They thus proceeded till they were met, probably as they descended the Mount of Olives toward the city, by the people coming from Jerusalem. They too were bearing branches of palm-trees, and they fell in with the procession. And the whole multitude of the disciples began to rejoice and to praise God for all the mighty works which they had seen. And they that went before, and they that followed, cried, "Hosanna to the Son of David! Blessed is he that cometh in the name of the Lord! Blessed be the coming kingdom of our father David! Hosanna in the highest!" Thus they went forward to Jerusalem.

Little did the multitude know what was passing in the thoughts of him whom they were thus honoring. Little did they understand how far he was from sharing the feelings and purposes by which they were impelled. In the midst of the triumph, the central figure of the whole, to whom all eyes and hearts turned, he was borne along passively, taking no part in the scene of which he was chief part. There was nothing to him exhilarating in the shouts or the gladness of the people; there was nothing to him glorious in this princely approach to the capital of the nation. He looked far beyond it all. He saw the truth and knew the future. And as the procession rolled on from the Mount of Olives and across the valley, he fixed his eyes on the guilty city, and wept at the ruin which was about to overtake it. "O that thou hadst known," he exclaimed, "even thou, at least in this thy day, the things that belong to thy peace! But now they are hidden from thine eyes."

As this remarkable assemblage drew near, it is no wonder that, as Matthew expresses it, all the city was moved, saying, "Who is this?" And the people answered, "This is Jesus of Nazareth, the Prophet of Galilee." Thus they proceeded into the gate, and wound up the steep ascent, and conducted Jesus to the temple.

The Pharisees and priests could ill bear this outbreak of popular enthusiasm. They said among themselves, "Ye perceive how we prevail nothing; the world is gone out after him." Some of them went to Jesus on the road, and attempted to persuade him to put an end to the commotion. But he replied, "I tell you if these should hold their peace, the stones would immediately cry out." After he had arrived in the temple, and the very children, seeing his miracles and catching the feeling of the crowd, shouted, "Hosanna to the son of David," the priests and scribes could not conceal their displeasure, and expressed it to him. "Hearest thou what these say?" "Yea," answered he, "have ye never read, Out of the mouth of babes and sucklings thou hast perfected praise?" Thus on all sides his malicious enemies were baffled. It was impossible for them, at such a moment, to execute their purpose.

Another occurrence was adapted still further to mortify them. Some Greeks, who, being probably proselytes to the Jewish faith, had come up to the festival, expressed to Philip a desire to be introduced to Jesus. They entertained the common expectations respecting the Messiah, and probably hoped, by attaching themselves to him, to share in the advantages of the kingdom, which, they judged from the events of the morning, was about being set up. Philip and Andrew made known to Jesus their request. Whether he granted it, and had an interview with the Greeks, is not said.

But their request excited in his mind a strong image of the glory to which he was appointed, and the sufferings through which he must reach it. The hour is come, said he, that the Son of man should be glorified. Not, however, by such glory as these Greeks expect, and which they desire to share. It is only through death that he is to obtain it, as the grain must perish in the earth, before it can bear fruit. And those who would share it must be ready like him to give up life.

As he thus spoke, he became agitated with the thoughts of dreadful suffering which rushed upon his mind. The Evangelist has not concealed it, for he would have the disciples in all ages know that their Master felt his own trials, and could therefore sympathize with them in theirs. He gave utterance to his feelings. "Now is my soul troubled; — and what shall I say? Father, save me from this hour!" It is uncertain whether these last words are to be considered as actually expressing a prayer, or whether they are simply a question; — Shall I say, Father, save me from this hour? In either case they strongly indicate the trouble of his soul. It was but momentary. He immediately checked it, and added, "But for this cause came I to this hour. Father, glorify thy name!" A voice from heaven immediately replied, "I have both glorified it, and will glorify it again." The by-standers were struck with surprise. Some thought it the voice of an angel, some said it only thundered. Jesus warned them that it was a voice intended for them; that now all unbelief was inexcusable, and judgment would overtake those who should reject him. He was about to triumph over the powers of the world, and his very death should give him universal dominion. So naturally did his mind rise to magnificent thoughts, even when the image of his sufferings pressed upon him most heavily! But the people, who were wedded to their old notions and would not open their minds to any change, asked him how he could talk of dying if he were the Messiah; for they had been taught to believe that that person would abide forever. Jesus replied, that this was no moment for captious cavilling; they yet had the light and might use it; it would soon be withdrawn, and darkness and ruin might overtake them. He entreated them to walk by it while they possessed it.

Thus passed the first day of his final visit to Jerusalem. It began in acclamation and triumph. It saw him hailed by the multitudes of the people, and led in honor to the city and the temple. To the hopes of his followers, all was bright and prosperous. His enemies were silenced, the people were full of enthusiasm in his favor, the temple was ringing with their hosannas, and even the Gentiles were crowding to do him homage.

Whatever then he might have meant when he talked of suffering and death, it was plain to his friends now that no such evils were to be feared; and they were ready to congratulate themselves on the close of their toils and the fulfilment of their hopes. But the Messiah himself knew better. He saw that all this show of honor was founded in mistake, and that as soon as the actual truth should be known, it would be withdrawn. There was very little faith among the people, which would survive the disappointment of their present excited expectations. Many, it is true, even among the chief priests, secretly believed in him; but they would not acknowledge it, because they would then be excommunicated. All this he knew; therefore the delusive promises of the day did not move him. Above all, he knew that the great work of benevolence which he was sent by the Father to perform could be accomplished only through his death. He had neither the thought nor the wish to shun it.

When the evening approached, he withdrew from the city with his disciples, and retired to Bethany. John says, "he did hide himself from them"; and we may suppose that his object was to escape, for the present, both the pursuit of his enemies, and the unreasonable excitement of the people. He continued to seek this retirement every evening to the close of his life.

John xii. 37.

CHAPTER XVII.

EVENTS OF THE SECOND AND THIRD DAYS.—VARIOUS DISCOURSES OF JESUS IN THE TEMPLE.—HIS PROPHECY OF THE DESTRUCTION OF JERUSALEM.

THE next day was Monday, and our Lord returned in the morning to Jerusalem. On his way thither occurred one of the striking incidents which contributed to give the present week so fearful a solemnity. Seeing a fig-tree at some distance, which had an appearance of bearing fruit, he went to it, but found none. In the hearing of his disciples, he commanded it to continue barren forever; and it withered away, so that the next morning it was observed by those who passed by it. This was a significant act, like some of those of the ancient prophets, designed as an emblematical representation of the decay which awaited the Jewish state in consequence of its unfaithfulness. It was putting in a visible form, if we may so say, the parable which he had before spoken, of the husbandman who had long looked in vain for fruit upon his tree, and therefore commanded it to be cut down.

Matthew xxi. 18. Mark xi. 12.

On reaching the temple, he now, as he had done at the last Passover, cleared its courts of the buyers and sellers, and reproved those who thus turned the house of prayer into a den of thieves. At the intermediate festivals, he had left them undisturbed; probably because his enemies were too active and powerful, and he could scarcely, with all his caution, escape them. But now his time was come, he was ready to end his work, and the present feeling of the people was such as to screen him from all ill consequences. So that although, when the rulers heard of this act, they thought to seize him, they found the state of the popular mind such that they dared not attempt it. They could not find what they might do, says Luke, for all the people were very attentive to hear him.

At evening he again left the city, and spent the night at some retired place in the neighborhood.

On Tuesday morning he returned to Jerusalem. On the way they passed by the withered fig-tree; and our Lord took the opportunity of impressing the twelve with the importance and worth of that undoubting faith, on which the power of working miracles depended. No work, he assured them, would be impossible to them who would ask in faith, and nothing would be denied them;—an assurance of great importance to them in the arduous and discouraging labors on which they were entering. They needed it; and in the miraculous powers which attended them wherever they went, their Lord's remarkable promise was literally fulfilled. To his disciples of the present day it does not literally apply; but in its *spirit* it holds good. Every one who prays in humble and hearty faith receives an inward spiritual blessing, worth as much to his soul as an outward miracle.

On arriving at the temple, as he walked among the porticos, conversing and teaching, he was addressed by certain of the chief priests and elders, who came to him, probably, as a deputation from the Sanhedrim. They had been prevented from executing their decree against him, by the strong feeling in his favor which existed among the people. It became necessary, therefore, to have some plausible pretext for an accusation, or their design would be defeated. With this view, they appointed deputies to put to him the question, in the hearing of the people in the temple, "By what authority doest thou these things, and who gave thee this authority?" They hoped to make use of his answer to entangle him with the Roman power. Jesus perceived their design, and foiled it by his reply. He said that he would tell them, if they would tell him their opinion of John's baptism; was it from heaven, or of men? This question they declined answering, because they

Matthew xxi. 23. Mark xi. 27. Luke xx. 1.

could not do it without committing themselves. He consequently refused to answer their insidious interrogation. He did not stop there. In the presence of the people to whom they had hoped to expose him, he pronounced a severe censure of their inconsistent disregard of the Baptist's instructions. He then recited that solemn parable in which he describes the various dispensations of God which had been abused by the Jewish people, the sending of his Son in hope that he would be reverenced, and the doom that awaited his rejection. They could not fail to perceive that he had aimed this parable against them, and they would gladly have seized him. But such was the crowd of people who were eagerly listening to him, that they dared not make the attempt.

They still, however, did not desist from their design of entangling him in his talk, that they might find whereof to accuse him. They accordingly, in the course of the day, sent to him another deputation, consisting of Pharisees and Herodians. These were to "feign themselves just men," says Luke, "and take hold of his words, that so they might deliver him to the power and authority of the governor." They accordingly addressed him with apparent respect, and in very complimentary terms asked his judgment on

Matthew xxii. 15. Mark xii. 12. Luke xx. 20.

the question, whether it were lawful to pay tribute to the Roman Emperor. Who the Herodians were, is not certainly known. Various opinions have existed in regard to them. They probably derived their name from Herod the Great, and were a sect partly religious and partly political. They probably advocated the cause of the Romans, and were averse to all opposition to their authority. The question which they put to Jesus was one from which it was difficult to escape; and although they had had many proofs of his wisdom and caution, they fancied that now they should successfully entrap him. They did not consider his power of penetrating beyond the appearance, and discerning the motives and thoughts of men. He perceived their hypocrisy, and foiled their cunning. "Why tempt ye me, ye hypocrites?" he said; "show me the tribute-money." They brought him a piece. "Whose image and superscription are these?" he asked. "Cæsar's," they replied. Then, said he, "Render unto Cæsar the things that are Cæsar's, and unto God the things that are God's." This admirable answer has passed into a proverb. When the questioners heard it, they marvelled at it, say the Evangelists; and, finding that they could not take hold of his words before the people, they held their peace and departed.

But there were other cavillers who pressed

upon him. Certain Sadducees, a sect who denied the doctrine of a resurrection, and held that there is no such thing as angel or spirit, came to him with a perplexing question about the future state. There was an air of self-satisfied cunning in their manner of proposing it, which showed that they really supposed they had brought this great teacher of immortality into an inextricable difficulty. But they had only given him an opportunity to expose the shallowness of their wisdom, and to explain, that in the future life they neither marry nor give in marriage, but are as the angels of God in heaven. The listening people were astonished and delighted at his reply. Some of the scribes exclaimed, "Master, thou hast said well." And one of them, pleased with what he heard, asked him which he considered to be the greatest commandment of the law. In reply to this question, Jesus quoted from the Old Testament, "Thou shalt love the Lord thy God with all thy heart, and with all thy soul, and with all thy mind, and with all thy strength, and thy neighbor as thyself"; adding, "there is no commandment greater than these." The scribe heartily assented to this. Upon which Jesus, as ready to commend the honest as to expose the hypocritical, said to him, "Thou art not far from the kingdom of God."

Meantime the Pharisees, pleased at his silencing their old opponents the Sadducees, had gathered round him again. He turned to them with a question on the great and engrossing subject of the expected Messiah. These bigoted men professed to understand fully the prophecies concerning him, and were obstinately confident in their notions respecting his character. They were particularly anxious at this moment to keep the people persuaded of the correctness of their own views. Jesus wished to show them, that, after all, they were ignorant, and to expose them for their presumption. He therefore asked, "What think ye of the Messiah? Whose son is he?" They answered, "David's." "But David calls him Lord," replied he; "how then is he his son?" To this they made no reply. They could make none, so long as they insisted that the Messiah was to be a temporal prince. It was only by acknowledging that his was a spiritual kingdom, and his authority that of a religious sovereign, that they could explain his superiority to David. But this they would not do. They would not open their eyes to their error. They were silenced; but they refused to be convinced. Yet as they found it vain to argue with him, and perceived that the more they strove to entangle him, the more they were themselves perplexed and exposed, they from that time asked him no more questions.

But the common people, says Mark, heard him gladly; and he immediately turned to them, and, in strong and pointed language, warned them against the example and influence of those unworthy men. As they were authorized religious teachers, their lessons should be observed; but their personal example should be shunned; they were hypocritical, ambitious, and oppressive. Then, boldly turning to the men themselves, in the presence and hearing of the people, he denounced them in a searching and solemn address, than which nothing so fearfully tremendous has been recorded in the history of eloquence. Its boldness, its personality, its prophet-like tone of urgent, yet unimpassioned rebuke, impart to it such a power, that it can hardly be read without trembling, and must have made it unspeakably awful in the delivery. It seems to have been listened to in death-like silence. No one presumed to interrupt it, or reply to it.

The next words uttered by him, as recorded by the Evangelists, stand in striking and beautiful contrast to those of this address. He was sitting where he could observe the people depositing their offerings in the treasury for the use of the temple. He saw a poor widow come with the rest, and put in the trifling sum of two mites, — amounting in value to a little more than half a cent. He

Matthew xxiii. 1. Mark xii. 37. Luke xx. 45.

bade his disciples notice it. And they must have felt how much worthier is humble goodness than worldly honor or wealth, when they heard him commend this poor woman as having made the richest offering; others had but given something from the midst of abundance, while she, from the midst of penury, had given her all.

As they were leaving the temple, some of the disciples called their Master's attention to the magnificence and riches of that noble building, with its beautiful stones and splendid offerings. It was indeed a sight well worthy of admiration. It had been rebuilt by Herod with great splendor, and for more than forty years had been receiving continual additions to its ornaments and wealth. Its spacious courts were paved with marble; its extensive porticos were supported by marble pillars; its massy gates were coated with gold and silver; and it was, on the whole, one of the most admirable buildings ever known. It stood on the summit of the holy mountain, two sides of which had been built up, from the valley below, with perpendicular walls of huge white stones, to the height, in some places, of three hundred cubits. Some of the stones are said, by Josephus, to have measured twenty-five cubits in length, eight in height, and twelve in breadth. A cubit is equal to about a foot and a half. It is no won-

Matthew xxiv., xxv. Mark xiii. Luke xxi.

der that the disciples looked with admiration on a building thus remarkable for its situation, its wealth, its beauty, and its strength. But Jesus, instead of responding to their remark, replied, "Verily I say unto you, there shall not be left here one stone upon another which shall not be thrown down."

They proceeded on their way, went out of the city, and seated themselves on the Mount of Olives. Jerusalem lay directly before them, as it were beneath their feet. It was probably toward the close of the day; and the setting sun shone bright upon its towers and pinnacles, its holy temple and gorgeous palaces. The disciples had been musing of what their Lord had said of its destruction; and now, as they sat looking upon it in its beauty, they came to him and inquired when this destruction should take place, and by what signs they might know of its approach; or, as they expressed it, "the sign of his coming and the end of the world," meaning the Jewish world, or dispensation. For they believed that the Messiah was to establish a new dispensation or age, by which that of Moses would be brought to an end.

Jesus replied to their question at great length. He began with warning them not to be deceived by false Messiahs, who would arise, and lead away many. Then he told them of the rise of commotions and wars, and finally of the desolation of the city by the Roman arms. He prophesied respecting all these things with minuteness, and assured them that they should all take place during that generation; as in fact came to pass with wonderful exactness. He urged them to watch and be prepared. He admonished them, by solemn and striking figures and parables, of the necessity of fidelity and perseverance. He pictured forth their duty and responsibility under the images of the thief in the night, of the ten virgins, and of the talents intrusted to the servants. And so passing from image to image, from one solemn topic of warning and exhortation to another, he led them on to the day of final retribution and eternal judgment; he left the form of parable and figure, and spoke in plain terms of the great last day; he painted to them the process of the judgment, described the characters of the blessed and the rejected, and repeated the awful sentence of final bliss and woe.

Nothing can be more impressive than this portion of our Lord's instructions, addressed primarily to his little band of followers on Olivet, but of unspeakable interest to all in every age. From their manner, it seems probable, that, although they were begun "privately," in presence of the twelve, or perhaps of only four of them, yet many persons collected around him before they were concluded, and they formed a public discourse. It adds to the interest with which we read it, to reflect that it was his last public discourse. With these words of fearful warning, and this affecting picture of the final judgment, he closed his ministry. On the Mount of Olives, over against the temple, in full view of the city for which he had toiled and prayed, over which he had lamented and wept, and in which and for which he was to suffer, were uttered the last public counsels of his holy and benevolent voice. But few heard them then, and fewer still understood them and treasured them up. But they have since been repeated to thousands and millions in all the languages of man. They have sunk deep into the hearts of countless multitudes, who heard not the Saviour's voice on earth, but who have learned to love and obey him, and long to be united with him in heaven. And when that great day arrives, many will undoubtedly receive his welcome, whose steps were led into the way of life and glory by this description of the judgment with which he closed his ministry among men.

When he had done speaking, he reminded his disciples that it was now but two days to the Passover, when he was to be betrayed and put to death.

From the Mount of Olives they then departed,

and retired to Bethany. In the evening a supper was made for him there,* in the house of Simon, "the leper," as he is called. He probably had been cleansed from his disease by Jesus, and showed him this hospitality from a feeling of gratitude and friendship. Lazarus was one of the company. His sisters also were present, and Martha served. During the repast, Mary gave a new proof of that affectionate devotion to her Lord which she had before exhibited. She had probably heard him speak, in the solemn way which impressed his followers, of his approaching sufferings and death. She was deeply affected by it. And, under the influence of her feelings, she came to him, as he sat at supper, with an alabaster box of precious perfume of spikenard, and poured it upon his head. John says, that she also poured it on his feet, and wiped them with her hair. This, according to the notions of that part of the world, was doing him a high and peculiar honor. It was the second time that it had been offered him in the course of his ministry.

Matthew xxvi. 6. Mark xiv. 3. John xii. 2.

* It might be inferred from John's account, that this took place several evenings previous, viz. on our Lord's first arrival in Bethany. But as both Matthew and Mark say it was two days before the passover, I have placed it here; understanding John not to speak of the time, but simply to state that they made the supper "*there.*" Otherwise we should have two suppers and two anointments precisely alike the same week.

But there were some present now, who felt, as the Pharisee did on the former occasion,* no sympathy with the deep reverence and affection which prompted the act. Judas, with others of the company, exclaimed against the extravagance and wastefulness of the deed. "It might have been sold," said they, "for three hundred denarii" [about forty-five dollars], "and given to the poor." Their pretended regard for the poor was ill-timed. No one had more of it than Jesus; but he felt that, in this instance, the expenditure was virtuous: it was the offering of sacred and reverential affection, excited by the approach of his death and the feeling that the opportunity of showing him honor would soon be past. He therefore defended her against the attack of the cavillers, — not only justifying, but applauding her; and assured them, that, wherever his Gospel should be preached, this deed of love should be celebrated.

Judas appears to have felt the rebuke keenly. He was probably at once mortified and angered. He knew how false were his own motives. He had not spoken from any charitable purpose, but for reasons simply selfish and criminal. He was the keeper of the common purse, and would have been glad to fill it with this goodly sum, that he might take from it what his dishonest hand de-

* See page 117.

sired. Perceiving himself detected, and the more angry at the reproof, as bad men are apt to be, because aware that he deserved it, he went immediately to the chief priests, and offered to betray his Master into their hands.

This was not the only instigating cause; others were unquestionably working in his evil mind; but this furnished the occasion. He was probably instigated to the treachery in part by cupidity, and the desire to secure the pecuniary reward. He had already, if we may judge from John's calling him a thief, robbed the purse of the little band, and doubtless, on this account, felt uneasy in their company, and ill-disposed toward them, as one is apt to do toward those whom he has wronged. His base and selfish mind, too, could have little sympathy with the severe and exalted character of his Master. He was disappointed in the ambitious expectations he had cherished. He could not readily exchange the honors at which he had been grasping for the defeat and disgrace which were now threatening him. And as the time drew near when even his Master had assured him there was hope no longer, he resolved to secure safety to himself, at any cost, and not lose everything in the inevitable ruin. It is not easy, perhaps, to enter fully into the motives which impelled him. Selfish, coarse, and

Matthew xxvi. 14. Mark xiv. 10. Luke xxii. 3.

dishonest habits of mind and life are sufficient to account for his conduct. If he had resisted the influence of his Lord's society and character to change them, it is not strange that he was capable of any baseness. If he could live with Jesus, and not be transformed, he was just the man to betray him. And if he had been revolving it in his mind, the offence he received at Simon's table was just the thing to goad him to the act.

Nothing could be more acceptable to the ruling powers, probably nothing more unexpected, than this offer of one of the familiar adherents of Jesus to aid them in their designs. Their chief obstacle was thus removed. They had long resolved to take him and put an end to his course. They had issued a proclamation for information respecting him. They had attempted to seize him. But they had always found him during the day surrounded by crowds of admiring listeners, and had not dared to lay their hands on the venerated prophet. "They feared the people." Again and again, also, they had tried to circumvent him in his conversation, and lay hold of some words for which he might be brought to prosecution. But these attempts had resulted in their own shame. They were thus wholly at a loss how to proceed. More than one meeting of the great council seems to have been held; and "they consulted how they might take Jesus by craft, and put him to death." But they effected nothing till Judas appeared before them, and proposed to lead them to him in his retirement; that is, as Luke expresses it, "in the absence of the multitude." This was precisely what they desired; and they contracted with him to do it for thirty pieces of silver, probably shekels, and equal in value, therefore, to about fourteen dollars and seventy cents. For this paltry reward did the miserable man blacken himself with infamy and guilt.

CHAPTER XVIII.

THE PASSOVER.—THE LORD'S SUPPER INSTITUTED.—JESUS CONVERSES AND PRAYS WITH THE APOSTLES.

THE feast of the Passover began on Thursday. On the morning of that day, the disciples inquired of Jesus where they should prepare for the evening festival. As none of them were inhabitants of Jerusalem, they must depend on the hospitality of some of the citizens for accommodation; and as, at this season, the houses were freely thrown open to the visitors from the country, there could be no difficulty in finding a place. Jesus directed them to the house of a person whom he pointed out, probably one of his followers, who had a large upper room ready furnished; and directed Peter and John to go thither, and make ready for the evening.

Their principal duty was to prepare the paschal lamb. This it was necessary for them to take to the temple, and slay before the altar with their own hands. One of the priests received the blood in a vessel, and it was poured out at the bottom

Matthew xxvi. 17. Mark xiv. 12. Luke xxii. 7.

of the altar. The fat was consumed on the altar. The time prescribed in the law for doing this was "at even, at the going down of the sun." Josephus says that it was done between the ninth and eleventh hours; that is, between three and five o'clock in the afternoon. After that, the lamb was to be roasted whole, not even a bone being allowed to be broken, and to be entirely eaten before morning.

The manner of conducting the supper appears to have been somewhat as follows. The lamb was placed upon the table, together with bitter herbs, unleavened bread, and a sauce called *charoseth*, in which the herbs and bread were dipped when eaten. This sauce was composed of dates, figs, and other fruits, beaten together, and is said to have been designed to represent the clay or mortar used by the Israelites in making bricks in Egypt. The party being assembled at table, not sitting, but reclining on couches, and leaning on the left arm, the master of the family poured out a cup of wine and water, gave thanks, and distributed it to all present. In the same way he afterward took a piece of the unleavened bread, pronounced a blessing, and distributed it. Toward the close of the meal a third cup of wine was drunk, called *the cup of blessing*. The ceremony was ended with a fourth, and by singing certain Psalms, namely, the cxvi., cxvii., cxviii.

We shall find traces of this order in the account of the last supper as observed by Jesus.

When the hour arrived, Jesus and the twelve sat down together. It was usual to assemble in family parties; but, in the present instance, there was a stronger bond than that of kindred to draw these friends together. It was possibly to this circumstance that Jesus alluded, when he said to his disciples, that he had exceedingly desired to keep this Passover in their company; not with his mother and kinsmen, but with his own chosen few. It might remind them of his having formerly said, that he regarded those as most truly his relatives who were most devoted to his Father's will.

It was probably in taking their places at the table that the contest for precedency, which is mentioned by Luke, arose among the disciples, — "a strife which should be accounted greatest." Jesus rebuked the unseasonable rivalry, reminded them that *place* was no true indication of worth, that he himself had been with them as a servant, and that it should be enough for them, who had continued with him through his trials, to know that they should share the honors of his kingdom at last.

Being placed at the table, he expressed to them his satisfaction at thus meeting them. He had

Luke xxii. 24.

greatly desired it, he said, because it would be the last opportunity. Then, taking the cup of wine, with which it was customary to begin the ceremony, he gave thanks, and distributed it among them.

He then rose from his couch, laid aside his upper robe, girded himself with a towel, and, taking a basin of water, proceeded to wash the disciples' feet. This service was usually performed by menials; and accordingly, when he came to Peter, that ardent apostle, unwilling to allow such condescension in his Master, cried out, "Thou shalt never wash my feet." "If I wash thee not," replied Jesus, "thou hast no part with me." Peter immediately went to the other extreme: "Lord, not my feet only, but my hands and my head." The answer of Jesus shows how strongly his mind was affected by the sad circumstance that one of his own twelve would betray him. He that has already bathed, he said, needs only to wash his feet, for he is clean; ye, therefore, are clean; "but not all," he added, as the thought of Judas came over him.

Resuming his place at the table, he explained to them, that he had thus been setting them an example of humility which they ought to follow. He probably had in mind what had passed before supper, and in this striking way endeavored to

John xiii. 1.

impress permanently on their hearts his lessons of humility and love.

As the supper proceeded, his mind again turned to the catastrophe, which was near. He was troubled in spirit, and said, "Verily I say unto you, one of you is about to betray me." The disciples looked at each other doubtingly and in amazement. Then they began to inquire among themselves whom he could mean. Then, unable to satisfy themselves, they asked him, one after another, "Is it I?" "Is it I?" The nearest of them to Jesus was John. He is called "the disciple whom Jesus loved," and is said to have lain in his bosom, because he reclined by his side on the couch. Peter beckoned to him, that he should ask who it was. John accordingly put the question in a whisper; and Jesus answered by giving him a sign; — it was that person to whom he should give the piece of bread which he had dipped in the Passover sauce; for this is what is meant by *the sop* in the Testament. He gave it to Judas. That wretched man seems to have borne this unexpected danger of exposure with a bold face. He did not betray himself in any way to his wondering companions. He even had the assurance to ask, with the rest, "Lord, is it I?" Jesus must have answered him in a voice not to be overheard by the others, for they did not learn

Matthew xxvi. 21. Mark xiv. 18. Luke xxii. 21. John xiii. 21.

that he was the man. At length, however, either because he could bear it no longer, or because the hour on which he had agreed with the Sanhedrim had come, he rose from the table and left the room. As he went out, Jesus said to him, "That thou doest, do quickly." It is remarkable that his departure excited no suspicion in the minds of the other disciples. They merely supposed, that, as Judas held the common purse, he had received directions to purchase what was necessary for the feast, or to give something to the poor. This last supposition of theirs, it has been remarked, shows that it was a custom with Jesus to distribute charity in this way.

It is not perfectly clear at what period Judas left the room, — whether before the supper was finished, or not until its close. Different opinions have been entertained on the point. From a comparison of the accounts of Matthew and John, it seems probable that he left in the midst. From Luke it might be inferred that he remained to the last. But as this writer was not present on the occasion, it appears better to arrange the narrative according to the testimony of the two former, who were eye-witnesses.

When Judas had gone, our Lord again adverted to his sufferings in terms similar to those which he had used when the Greeks applied to him in the temple. "Now is the Son of man glorified, and God is glorified in him." He then, addressing his disciples affectionately as his "children," added, that his time was at hand, that he must shortly go from them, and entreated them to love one another as he had loved them. Peter, not perceiving his meaning, asked him whither he was going. Jesus repeated, that at present he could not follow him, but should do so at some future time. Still Peter did not understand; and fearing that Jesus might say this because doubtful of his courage or fidelity, he exclaimed, "Lord, why can I not follow thee now? I will lay down my life for thy sake." "Wilt thou lay down thy life for my sake?" said his Master; "verily I say unto thee, the cock will not crow till thou hast denied me thrice." The warm-hearted apostle took fire at this, and cried out, "Though I die with thee, yet will I not deny thee." The other ten joined him in this declaration. But Jesus assured them that they would all take offence and be scattered from him before morning. Peter still insisted that, however it might be with the others, it should not be so with him. Jesus answered that they were about to go through a peculiarly severe trial; that for him he had especially prayed, that his faith might not fail; and bade him, when recovered from the shock it should receive, strengthen that of his brethren.

Matthew xxvi. 31. Mark xiv. 27. Luke xxii. 31. John xiii. 36.

In relating the severer trials they were to encounter, he further said, that the days were past when they could go from place to place as they had done, without purse, or sandals, or sword, secure from assault and evil, and welcomed wherever they went. The times had changed. He himself was to suffer as a malefactor, and they would henceforth be subjected to want and perils, such as would make it necessary to provide for their own sustenance, and to be ready to part with their clothing for the sake of a sword. The disciples, still in the dark, fancied that he recommended them to arm themselves, and said, "Here are two swords." He replied, "It is enough"; as if he had said, Very well, — with a sigh of disappointment to find that their obtuse minds were still blind to the real posture of affairs.

As the ceremony proceeded, Jesus took the unleavened cake, and, agreeably to the usage of the occasion as already described, broke it, and divided it among the disciples. But he told them that henceforth its meaning and object were to be changed. It was no longer to be eaten in commemoration of their fathers in Egypt. They must regard it as a memorial of himself, and consecrate the occasion to his memory. So also he took the cup of wine, which it was customary, at the close of the supper, to bless and distribute among the company. This, too, he told them, was henceforth to commemorate a greater event than the deliverance from Egyptian bondage. It was to denote the shedding of his blood for the ratification of a new covenant, and was to be drunk in memory of himself. Thus he changed for them the character of this ancient festival; he converted it from its original national purpose into a purely spiritual commemoration of himself. He thus established that simple but touching observance which is a peculiar rite of his religion, and which has been cherished by believers in all ages since, dear and hallowed as the memory of its Founder.

It was impossible that this act should not deeply affect the minds of the disciples. He had often spoken to them of late on the subject of his approaching death; but they had not understood him, nor believed that he was to die. But now, when he spoke of treachery, and formally charged them to keep this feast thenceforward as a memorial of his death, — declaring that he never should again partake of it with them, — they must have been filled with fearful forebodings and alarm. Jesus perceived their distress, and applied himself to console it. "Let not your hearts be troubled," said he; "ye believe in God, believe also in me." Let it comfort you to reflect, that I have only gone before you to my Father's house, and shall return to receive you thither, that we may at last be alway together. Still, however, their minds were not perfectly clear. Thomas and Philip and Judas, the brother of James, put questions to him, which showed that they were yet groping in the dark. He explained himself to them; reminded them how dear he was to the Father, and that therefore they should rather rejoice that he was going to him; assured them that they should not be left comfortless, that they should be objects of the Father's love and favor, and be blessed by the gift of the Holy Spirit. And finally he said, "Peace I leave with you; my peace I give unto you."

But his discourse did not consist wholly of words of comfort. The truest consolation is always found in the strength of virtuous principle and preparation for virtuous action; and it would have been of little avail to the apostles, that their present apprehensions were soothed, unless they had also been made to understand what was required of them, and nerved to bear the sufferings and do the work appointed them. They were going forth on the most important errand on which men had ever been commissioned. They were going into the midst of trials to which men had never been exposed. Everything was to depend on the constancy and fidelity with which they should execute their trust. Jesus felt that in vain

John xv., xvi.

had he begun an enterprise the most beneficent to man and the most glorious to God, unless it were prosecuted in his spirit. This spirit he labored to infuse into them. He strove to make them comprehend how much was depending on their feeling their connection to himself, and devoting themselves exclusively to his cause. He urged them to adhere to him in all affection and confidence, because they could otherwise have no strength and success, any more than a branch could live and bear fruit without connection with the vine. He urged them to adhere to one another in brotherly love, and thus to recommend their cause and their Master to the world. He pleaded with them the memory and example of his own love for them, and warned them against the ruinous consequences of remissness and unfaithfulness. At the same time, he did not disguise the perils to which this course would expose them; he told them that they had much opposition to encounter, and severe sufferings to endure. But they should not be unsupported. The spirit of God would be with them to guide, sustain, and bless them, and no request which they should make of the Father in his name would be denied them.

Much of this consoling and admonitory language appears to have been lost on the disciples at the time. There was still a mist before their eyes. They did not clearly see what he meant by "going to the Father." They whispered among themselves, inquiring what he could mean; and Jesus explained himself to them more perfectly. Still there remained much, the full import of which could enter their minds only when, some time afterward, the resurrection of their Lord and the gifts of the Spirit had opened their eyes to the true purposes of his mission, and the real character of their enterprise. Then the solemn, exciting, and soothing discourses of this painful evening must have come to their recollection with a sustaining and invigorating influence; and, mingled with the image of their gracious friend and the tones of his benignant voice, must have filled their hearts with the confidence and peace of which he spoke in the concluding words: "These words I have spoken unto you, that in me ye might have peace. In the world ye will have tribulation; but be of good cheer; I have overcome the world."

Having finished what he had to say to his disciples, Jesus lifted up his eyes, and prayed. He prayed for himself, for his apostles, for all his disciples, for his followers and his truth in all ages. He poured out his earnest and affectionate desires in a strain of supplication unspeakably pathetic and sublime. His beloved disciple has put his

John xvii.

prayer on record. In reading it we gain admittance into the soul of his Master; we feel how powerful and elevating is his truth. We are overcome with admiration, that one about to perish by a violent and ignominious death should exhibit this consciousness of an intimate union with the supreme Father, — should display this calm assurance that the grandest purposes of the Divine government were connected with his own fate, — should thus lift himself above the present time and present scenes, and speak of the invisible and eternal as if familiar with their glories. We know that no one before him had thus spoken; and, as we listen to his words, we exclaim, "Truly this was the Son of God."

CHAPTER XIX.

JESUS RETIRES TO GETHSEMANE. — IS APPREHENDED. — IS CONDEMNED BY THE SANHEDRIM. — PETER DENIES HIM.

It is not perfectly clear whether the whole of the scene just related took place in the room in which the Passover supper was eaten; or whether a large portion of the last discourse of Jesus were not held in the open air as he was proceeding with his disciples toward the Mount of Olives. The latter is thought by many to be the more probable; and they conceive that the image which he used of the vine and its branches was suggested by the vineyards through which they passed on their way.

However this may have been, they left the city, as had been their custom every night, and retired over the brook Kedron to the Mount of Olives. This brook runs through the bottom of the valley which lies between Olivet and Jerusalem. After crossing it, they proceeded for about half a mile, when they came to a garden called

Matthew xxvi. 36. Mark xiv. 32. Luke xxii. 39. John xviii. 1.

Gethsemane, lying just at the foot of the mountain. It seems to have been a favorite resort of Jesus, being probably attached to the house of some one of his followers, and well situated for retirement. Here they had hitherto been safe from pursuit; but Judas, who had always been with them, knew the place, and he had now left them for the purpose of conducting to it the officers of the Sanhedrim.

The Passover was always celebrated at the full of the moon. And nothing can well be more lovely than the moonlight night of that season of the year in that beautiful part of the world. But the hearts of this little company were too heavy to allow them to feel the beauty of external nature. On the minds of the disciples the events of the evening had left a vague but strong impression of grief and apprehension. To their Master's mind all was clear. He saw the whole reality. He knew exactly the horrors that were approaching. He felt them more and more as the hour drew nigh. Leaving the other disciples, he took Peter, James, and John to a more retired part of the garden. "My soul is exceeding sorrowful," said he, "even unto death; tarry ye here and watch with me." He went a little distance, and threw himself on his face, upon the ground, and prayed that, if it were possible, the hour might pass from him. "Abba! Father!"

he cried, "all things are possible unto thee; take away this cup from me! Nevertheless, not what I will, but what thou wilt." Three times, at intervals, he repeated this prayer. The struggle of feeling, Luke tells us, amounted to agony. The sweat poured from him like drops of blood, and he prayed more and more earnestly. He was not unanswered. An angel appeared from heaven, strengthening him. And he rose up, calm, strong, and ready to endure, with a fortitude which never for a moment shrunk back.

Meantime the disciples, overcome with excitement, fatigue, and grief, gave way to drowsiness and fell asleep. He returned to them again and again in the intervals of his own distress, hoping to find one word, at least, of sympathy, from those who loved him; but they were asleep. "Simon," said he, addressing the apostle who had been most forward in his promises of aid,— "Simon, sleepest thou? Couldst thou not watch with me one hour?" Then reminding them of their situation and perils, he urged them to watch and pray; for, however prepared they might be in disposition and heart, in body they were weak, and might be overcome when least expecting it. But they did not sufficiently comprehend either his situation or their own to be kept awake by it. They fell asleep again as soon as he turned away from them.

He had just roused them the third time, when lights were seen approaching, and the band of officers and soldiers entered the garden to apprehend him, with Judas at their head. This false disciple, adding insult to treachery, came boldly to his Lord, cried, "Hail, Master!" and kissed him. This was the sign by which his person was to be pointed out to the officers. "Judas," said the Saviour meekly, "betrayest thou the Son of man with a kiss?" Then, advancing to the company, he inquired, "Whom seek ye?" "Jesus of Nazareth," they replied; and when they found themselves in the presence of the person of whose power and goodness they had heard so much, they were struck with involuntary awe, and started back, and fell to the ground. He again spoke to them, and, begging them to permit his disciples to depart, surrendered himself into their hands.

The disciples, roused suddenly from their sleep, and perceiving the band of armed men, appear to have been amazed and panic-struck. Peter, always hasty, drew his sword, and wounded one of the men. But Jesus healed the wound with a touch, and rebuked the impetuous disciple; he reminded him that force could only lead to evil; that his submission was voluntary; that even now, if he should ask it, Heaven would interpose for his rescue; but that this would be inconsistent with the great purposes of God, for "how then should the Scriptures be fulfilled?" The other disciples offered no resistance. They appear to have stood by, passive and bewildered. They were taken by surprise, and obeyed the impulse of the moment, and fled. A few hours before they had declared, as they had doubtless felt, that they would abide by their Master to the last. But they did not know themselves so well as he did; and when the hour of which he had warned them came, they forgot their affection and their promises, and deserted him. They left their teacher, their benefactor, their friend, to pass alone, without sympathy, through the trying scenes of his extremity. Two ventured to follow him at a distance; but the others disappeared.

Jesus was led away, bound, to the presence of the Sanhedrim, by whose orders he had been apprehended.

This Council, the highest and most sacred court of the Jews, consisted of seventy persons, and is often intended in the New Testament when "the chief priests, elders, and scribes" are spoken of. Some argue that it was the same council with that constituted by Moses in the wilderness, continued down through all the changes of the nation; but it was, more probably, of a later origin. It had supreme authority in all matters peculiar to the Mosaic institutions, and was allowed to exercise it even under the dominion of the Romans.

The regular place of meeting of the Sanhedrim was in a circular hall of the temple, in the court of the priests. The Jews say, that, about forty years before the destruction of the city, the meetings ceased to be held in that place. On the present occasion, the venerable court assembled at the palace of the high-priest, Caiaphas, — the same who, at a former meeting, had recommended the policy of putting Jesus to death in order to save the nation from the displeasure of the Romans. The members of the council seem to have remained there during the night, awaiting the performance of Judas's promise. And there they were, when, in the darkness of the early morning, their officers arrived with the man whose life they had so long and so eagerly sought. They had in vain attempted to seize him during the day; the night was the only time, and it was a fit time, for their work of darkness.

Before these prejudiced men, — who had long ago resolved on his death, whose malice had become exasperated by his so long escaping them, and who were now probably more than ever excited because obliged to assemble at an unseasonable hour for fear of the people, — their innocent victim was brought in bound. The proceedings began with a show of moderation, but not as a fair trial would have begun. The high-priest interrogated the prisoner respecting his disciples and his doctrine. To this Jesus replied, that he had lived and taught publicly; what he had done was before the world; witnesses might easily be found to testify on this head; he was not himself the proper person to be inquired of. It shows the temper of the tribunal, that for this reply one of the officers was permitted to strike Jesus. Yet he had plainly done nothing but state the proper course of proceeding. If he was on trial, witnesses should be summoned.

A show was then made of calling witnesses. But it was not easy to find such as would answer the purpose. At length two men came forward, and declared that they had heard him say, "I am able to destroy the temple of God, and to build it in three days." Something like this he had said at the preceding Passover; and that must have been a faultless life indeed, from which nothing more could be gathered that would bear a criminal construction. As if this were a heinous offence, and nothing further need be required, the high-priest rose from his seat, and asked the prisoner what he had to reply. Jesus had already perceived how vain it was to speak, and remained silent. But it was necessary, if possible, to extort from his own mouth something which might serve to justify their proceeding against him. Therefore the high-priest said, "I adjure thee, by the living God, that thou tell us whether thou be the Christ, the Son of God." This was the regular form of a judicial oath. Jesus felt bound to reply; and declared that he was not only the Messiah, but that they should witness his glory and exaltation. Upon hearing this, the high-priest declared it to be blasphemy, rent his garments to express his horror, and appealed to the council that no further testimony was necessary. To this they all assented, and pronounced sentence of death. Then ensued a scene of outrage which would not be tolerated in the presence of any modern tribunal in the civilized world. He was buffeted, spit upon, derided, and the officers and servants made him their mockery and sport.

If we rightly understand the account, there was now a little pause in the doings of the council; for it is said to have come together again at daybreak, to consult as to the manner of carrying their sentence into execution. By the law of Moses, a person convicted of blasphemy should be stoned to death. But whether the council really did not now possess this power, which is uncertain, or whether they apprehended that the people would rise to prevent them, or whether they sought to gratify their malice by exposing him to a death more cruel and ignominious, — whichever the reason might be, they determined to carry him before the governor on a charge of sedition and treason.

During all this painful scene, no one had appeared for Jesus, no one had spoken for him. Only two of his disciples had even had the courage to follow him. One of these, generally supposed to be John, being known to the high-priest, had found easy admission to his house, and obtained admittance for Peter also. Where John placed himself, he has not told us. Peter mingled with the servants who were sitting around a fire in the hall, and hoped to escape notice while he observed what was going forward. What he saw and heard agitated and intimidated him; so that, when one person after another recognized him as a follower of Jesus, he stoutly denied it; and when at last the proof seemed to be growing stronger, and detection to be unavoidable, he a third time denied it with oaths. At this moment the cock crew, and the recollection of his Master's words and a sense of his own baseness rushed upon his mind. He looked toward Jesus, and met his eye fixed full upon him. He could not bear it. He rushed out, and burst into tears.

So fell the first and most ardent of the apostles. But he repented, and rose again, and obtained mercy, and lived to compensate for his temporary defection. Not so with that more unhappy man who had deliberately betrayed his Lord. He, indeed, sorrowed for his sin; but it was the sorrow of despair. When he found that Jesus was condemned, he was seized with remorse; he carried back the money to the priests, declaring that he had betrayed innocent blood; they derided him for his scruples; and he went away in a state of desperation, and destroyed himself.

CHAPTER XX.

JESUS IS BROUGHT BEFORE PILATE, AND CONDEMNED.

THE stated residence of the Roman governors of Judæa was Cesarea, a town on the sea-coast. At the great festivals they came to Jerusalem to enjoy the pomp of the occasion, and attend to the administration of justice. Pilate was accordingly now in the city. He had been governor for about five years; and was acquainted with the peculiarities of the people and of their institutions.

It was yet early in the morning, when the members of the council, removing from the house of Caiaphas, presented themselves with Jesus at the Prætorium, for so the palace of the governor was called. Jesus was led into the presence of Pilate; but his accusers remained without; for they could not enter the house of a Gentile without danger of contracting a pollution which would unfit them for participating in the festival. They could do a great injustice, but they would not endure a small defilement. So much stronger

Matthew xxvii. 11. Mark xv. 1. Luke xxiii. 1. John xviii. 28.

was their superstition than their principle. Accordingly they remained at the tribunal in front of the palace. The governors were accustomed to administer justice in the open air; and the tribunal was erected for that purpose on a pavement of mosaic.

The governor came out to them to inquire into the nature of the accusation; and, being probably desirous to get rid of an affair which he supposed to concern their own peculiar customs, directed them to take Jesus, and deal with him according to their law. They replied that it was not lawful for them to put any man to death. It has been a great question, whether this was true in its full extent, or whether they only meant to be understood as intimating that the offence of Jesus was against the Roman government, and not against their own institutions. They added what is to be considered as their formal indictment: "We found this man perverting the nation, and forbidding to give tribute to Cæsar, saying that he himself is Christ, a king." It was a charge of sedition and rebellion.

Pilate retired, and interrogated Jesus. He did not deny that he was king of the Jews; but he explained that his was a kingdom not of this world, and such as would not at all interfere with the kingdom of Cæsar; adding, that the great office which he had to discharge was that of establishing TRUTH. Pilate not understanding this, or thinking it nothing to the purpose, immediately went out again, and declared to his accusers that he found the prisoner innocent of all crime. This rendered them only the more fierce, as Luke expresses it; and, varying the terms of the accusation a little, they charged him with exciting sedition among the people, from Galilee to Jerusalem.

Finding Jesus to be a Galilean, Pilate sent him to Herod, who was at this time in the city, having come up to pass there the season of the festival. He doubtless felt relieved at the prospect of shifting off the responsibility of so delicate a case upon another magistrate.

Herod, as has appeared in the course of the history, had long been desirous of seeing the extraordinary prophet who had been so famous in his province; but Jesus had taken care to avoid him. The tetrarch was rejoiced to meet him at last, and strove to gratify his curiosity by inducing him to perform some such miracle as he had heard of, and by asking a variety of questions. But Jesus refused to answer the idle questioner. Herod was irritated; and, learning the nature of the accusations against him, insulted his royal pretensions by clothing him in a gorgeous robe, and sent him back to Pilate. This interchange of civilities was the means of restoring a good understanding between the two magistrates. It could not have occupied a great deal of time, especially if Herod and Pilate resided, as some have supposed, in different apartments of the great palace built by Herod the Great.

The governor was entirely satisfied that Jesus was innocent of the charges urged against him, and perfectly aware that they had been made maliciously. He was desirous, therefore, to discharge him. This desire was strengthened by a message brought to him from his wife, who had been troubled respecting Jesus in a dream, and who entreated him to "have nothing to do with that just man." When, therefore, the prisoner was brought back to him from Herod, he made another attempt to save him; not by directly exerting his authority in releasing him, — he had not moral courage enough for this, — but by appealing to the magnanimity of the accusers. It was customary for the governor to honor the feast by granting pardon to some criminal. He proposed that Jesus should receive this boon. But the chief priests and elders instigated the people to refuse the proposal. "Away with him," they cried, "and release to us Barabbas." Now Barabbas was a robber who had been convicted of sedition and murder. "What then," asked Pilate, "shall I do with Jesus, who is called Christ?" They cried out, "Crucify him!" The governor still parleyed. "Why?" said he, "what evil hath he done?" But the mob had become excited and impatient. Neither argument nor entreaty could avail. They only shouted the more loudly and fiercely, "Crucify him, crucify him!"

When Pilate perceived that expostulation was vain, and that there was danger of a serious tumult, he yielded; and to show that he did so reluctantly, he took a vessel of water, and publicly washed his hands, saying, "I am innocent of the blood of this just person; see ye to it." The infatuated people cried out, "His blood be on us and on our children!" Little did they guess the extent of the dreadful imprecation. It was followed, in the retributions of Providence, by calamities such as perhaps no other nation ever endured, by the ruin of their city and the dispersion of their people.

Crucifixion was the Roman punishment for sedition, and as such was demanded for Jesus. It was always preceded by scourging. To this preliminary cruelty the Saviour was now publicly subjected. He was then led back into the court of the Prætorium. The soldiers of the band upon duty there gathered around him, and in heartless sport derided and insulted him. In mockery of his regal title they clothed him in a robe of imperial purple, placed upon his head a crown which they had made of thorns, and put a reed into his shackled hands for a sceptre. They bowed the knee before him, and saluted him with, "Hail! King of the Jews!"

Pilate was still willing to make one more attempt to save him. He caused Jesus to be led out again, and, presenting him in his condition of wretchedness to the people, sought to move them to relent. He urged again, that he had found him guiltless of all offence. But the only answer he received was the hideous shout of "Crucify him, crucify him!" Pilate answered, "Take ye him and crucify him; for I find no fault in him." Finding the governor thus resolute to maintain his innocence, they replied that, however it might be with the charge of sedition, he deserved death, by the Jewish law, for his blasphemy; he had declared himself to be the Son of God. This was giving a new aspect to the affair. Pilate did not know what meaning the Jews attached to the title; but he believed, as the heathen did, that the sons of some of the deities were often found among men. He therefore went back to Jesus, who had been again withdrawn to the Prætorium, and asked him, with some uneasiness, who he claimed to be, and what was his origin. To this question, Jesus, who knew that enough had been already said, made no reply. Pilate then reminded him that he was in his power, and that his life or death

John xix.

might depend on his answer. Jesus answered, that the governor had that power only through Divine permission; and therefore, he added, — ready, as he ever was, to make allowance, — "he who delivered me unto thee hath the greater sin."

The result of this conversation was that Pilate returned to the people more than ever anxious to save his prisoner. But they still had one argument in reserve, — the displeasure of the Emperor. "If thou let this man go," they said, "thou art not Cæsar's friend." Pilate well knew the jealous and unreasonable temper of Tiberius, and that, if the Jews should make an unfavorable report of this proceeding, it might excite that tyrant to ruin him at once. He dared not meet the hazard. He sat down on the tribunal, caused Jesus to be brought before him, passed the sentence which his accusers had desired, and delivered him into their hands.

CHAPTER XXI.

THE CRUCIFIXION.

It is not easy for us, at the present day, to conceive the terrible suffering of a death by crucifixion, or to understand the disgrace which was attached to it. It was the most shameful, as well as cruel, of all modes of execution. It was reserved for the most abandoned malefactors and for slaves. When we speak of the disgrace of being condemned to the gallows, we present no picture of ignominy to be compared with that which pertained to crucifixion.

The form of the cross is familiar to us. But it is commonly represented as of a far greater altitude than really belonged to it. It was rarely more than ten feet in height. The upright beam, which was planted in the ground, was called *the tree;* and hence the Apostle Paul uses that name for the cross. Near the top it was crossed by a bar at right angles, on which was written the crime for which the person suffered. To the extremities of this his hands were fastened by nails driven through the palms. Thus the whole weight of his body was suspended by his hands, excepting as he partially sat on a small projecting piece of wood. His feet were nailed to the beam, but without anything to support them. In this torturing situation the poor sufferer hung for many hours, and died at last in indescribable agony. So terrible was the torment, that it became customary to give the victim an intoxicating drink for the purpose of deadening his feelings; and the executioners often hastened the time of death by suffocation or otherwise, especially if the struggle continued longer than a day.

This was the suffering to which the blessed Jesus was destined. No interval was allowed between the sentence and its execution. He was hurried away immediately, carrying on his shoulders the cross to which he was to be nailed; for it was part of the cruelty of this mode of punishment, that the condemned should bear his own instrument of torture. Thus he was led through the city by the unfeeling soldiers, and out of the western gate, on the side of the city opposite to the temple. It soon appeared that the watching and fatigue of the last day and night had rendered him incapable of sustaining the burden of his cross; and as he sunk under it, the soldiers seized upon Simon, a Cyrenian, who is commonly thought to have been one of the disciples, and

Matthew xxvii. 32. Mark xv. 21. Luke xxiii. 26. John xix. 17.

compelled him to carry his Master's burden. Mark speaks of two sons of this man by name, as if it had been accounted an honor to be the children of him who had thus helped his Lord in an hour of need.

The crowd of spectators, as might be expected, was immense. The whole male population of Judæa was assembled at the city, and the history and character of the sufferer were too well known not to excite a universal and intense interest. The inhabitants of the city, being under the immediate influence of the leading men, had never been friendly to him, and they undoubtedly composed the principal part of the mob which had crowded around the tribunal in the morning, and intimidated the governor. Many too, without doubt, who had joined in honoring him when they thought him the Messiah, on the preceding Sunday, now turned violently against him in revenge for their disappointment, when they fancied him proved to be an impostor. Still, however, it could not be that enemies alone attended the melancholy procession. Multitudes there must have been whose attachment for a matchless benefactor survived the disappointment of the day, and who now followed him with heavy hearts and tearful eyes to the place of his suffering.

It was about the third hour, or nine o'clock in the morning, when they arrived at the place of execution. This was a small eminence on the northwest side of the city, not far from the walls. It is commonly called Mount Calvary; but its elevation is so slight that it hardly deserves the name of a mountain. Here the Saviour was crucified in company with two malefactors, one on each side of him. The soldiers offered him the customary draught of stupefying ingredients; but he refused it; he would take nothing which should deaden his feelings or cloud his perception. He would die with his faculties in all their brightness.

The scene which followed is too painful to be dwelt upon. The soldiers sat down in sport at the foot of the cross, dividing part of his raiment among themselves, and throwing dice for his woven and seamless coat. The brutal mob, that crowded around, vented their enmity in cries of insult and derision. Even the priests and scribes and elders, men of distinction and dignity, joined in the mockery, and poured out their malignant revenge on the meek and patient sufferer. Nay, one of the malefactors, who hung groaning at his side, joined the dreadful ribaldry. But all this the meek and patient sufferer heeded not, except that it drew forth a prayer for their forgiveness. He seemed to have no ear for the cries that were filling the air. But to other things he was attentive, and exhibited the same readiness to think and feel for others which he had displayed in his days of power. When, during the painful progress from the city, he observed the women in the crowd lamenting, he turned to them and said, "Daughters of Jerusalem! weep not for me, but weep for yourselves and for your children." When one of the malefactors appealed to him for mercy, he answered him with ready words of encouragement and promise. When he looked round upon the crowd, and saw there, amid a group of weeping friends, his disconsolate mother, he remembered what she must endure at his loss, and felt for her bereaved and desolate loneliness. He turned therefore to his favorite disciple, John, who was standing with her, and charged him to regard her as his mother, — a charge which, John assures us, he faithfully observed, giving her a home in his own house.

At about noon, the day grew dark; not from an eclipse of the sun, for the moon was at the full. It was a supernatural obscurity, which extended over the land, and lasted for three hours. At that time the Saviour's sufferings had continued for six hours. They were now drawing toward a close; and, as it is usual for the pains of this death to be growing constantly more dreadful to the last, they appear to have increased in severity. He cried out, "My God, my God, why hast thou forsaken me?" They are the words which form the beginning of the twenty-second Psalm; and he is thought to have repeated them, in order to draw attention to a passage of Scripture so descriptive of his condition. He then complained of thirst, and a soldier put to his mouth a sponge soaked in vinegar. All was now over. He exclaimed, "It is finished!" and, devoutly addressing God with the words, "Father, into thy hands I commend my spirit!" he breathed his last.

Then occurred other prodigies to attest the dignity of the person who had suffered, and the interposition of a Divine hand. The veil of the temple was rent from top to bottom; the earth quaked; the rocks were torn asunder; the graves were opened; and some of the dead came back to life. It was impossible to mistake these signs. The centurion who presided at the execution exclaimed, "Truly this was the Son of God!" And the people who had come together, awe-struck and alarmed, smote their breasts, and returned.

It was the custom with the Romans to leave the bodies of crucified criminals exposed on the cross without burial; but they made an exception in Judæa, because the law of Moses commanded that all such should be buried before night. The Jews were particularly desirous that this should be done at the present time, because at the setting of the sun the Sabbath was to begin, and a

Sabbath during the Passover was a day of more than ordinary sacredness. The soldiers were accordingly directed to hasten the death of the sufferers by breaking the bones of their legs. But finding, to their surprise, that Jesus had already expired, they forbore to commit this violence on his body. One of the soldiers, however, from what motive we do not know, thrust a spear into his side. It was thus put beyond all doubt that he was actually dead; for the wound was followed by a mixed flowing of blood and water, which could have come only from the region about the heart. It was of great consequence to put this fact beyond question, because upon this must depend the all-important fact of the resurrection which followed.

The last hours of Jesus were not wholly unattended by the kindnesses of friends. Of the apostles, John at least, and perhaps others, were present at the crucifixion. So also were many of those devoted female friends who had accompanied him from Galilee. And now, when the last agony was past, two disciples from among persons of dignity and wealth obtained his body from the governor, that they might give it a decent and affectionate burial. These were Joseph of Arimathea and Nicodemus. They took the body of their departed friend, and, hastily preparing it for interment, conveyed it into a garden near the place of crucifixion, and placed it in a new tomb belonging to Joseph. The women from Galilee attended, and saw where he was laid. None of them imagined that they should ever behold his face again. And when they had placed a stone at the mouth of the cave, they felt that all they had most honored and loved was buried there forever.

But his enemies remembered what his friends had forgotten, — that he had spoken of rising again on the third day. Not that they expected any such event; but they feared that the disciples might remove the body, and pretend that he had risen. They therefore sealed the door of the sepulchre, and placed a guard of soldiers there to keep all secure.

And here, to all human appearance, was the close of expectations from Jesus of Nazareth. Executed as a criminal, his immediate followers dispersed, and a Roman guard watching over his tomb, the mind of man could not conjecture that he would ever again be heard of except as one of the many unsuccessful adventurers who had excited and disappointed the hopes of a credulous people. His enemies had completely triumphed. His adherents were wholly disheartened. Nothing can account for the revival of his cause and the spread of his religion, except that they were the special charge of a superintending Providence.

Most truly did Gamaliel declare, a few weeks afterward, that, if this enterprise had a human origin, it would come to naught. For all the power of man was exerted to overthrow it. That it was not overthrown proves it to have been upheld by the power of God.

CHAPTER XXII.

THE RESURRECTION AND ASCENSION.

THE Sabbath came, with its holy hours of worship and rest. The incense and the sacrifices were offered up in the temple, and its ample courts resounded with the tread of innumerable worshippers, and the voices of those who sang praise. There were no signs to show that the glory of Israel, the object of so many prophecies, the desire of all nations, the great benefactor of the human race, had just been rudely destroyed by the people whom he had come to bless. The festival went on, and the crowded city rejoiced. The religious leaders, wrapt up in their bigotry and self-importance, exulted in an achievement which was to bring down ruin upon them from the God whom they had offended; and the mass of the people, ignorant and blind, were content to have gratified their passions and the will of their superiors, little knowing that they had risen against their truest friend. Had they known it, they would not have crucified the Lord of glory.

But all were not thus. There were friends of

that holy and just one, who, though they were far from a full comprehension of his character, yet mourned him in the depths of their souls as the most excellent and admirable of beings. It is easy to judge what was the gloom of this day to them. To the eleven apostles especially, who had cause to feel shame for their desertion of him, as well as grief at his death, it must have been a day of unmixed sorrow and despair. Not a ray of light appears to have beamed upon their minds. He whom they had loved, trusted, and followed as the Redeemer of Israel, had been cut down by their side; and with him all hope, all gladness, had fled. They had no power, so stupefied were they by a calamity for which they were unprepared, to call up to mind the consolation and promises by which he had attempted to fortify them for this very hour. And, instead of rejoicing in the confidence of his revival, they could do nothing but deplore his loss.

Thus the Sabbath passed away, and the dawn of the first day of the week drew nigh. The affectionate women, who had accompanied Joseph and Nicodemus when they hastily deposited the body of their Master in the tomb, had waited anxiously for the dawn, that they might finish the rites of burial. They had prepared the customary spices and ointments, and with the first ray of

Matthew xxviii. Mark xvi. Luke xxiv. John xx.

light after the holy time was passed, they made haste to return and complete their mournful office. So little did they anticipate the event which was about to take place!

They arrived at the tomb, and to their astonishment found it open. The stone had been rolled away from its mouth. They entered it, and to their yet greater amazement found it empty. While perplexed at this, they were addressed by a person in white raiment, whom Matthew describes as the angel who had rolled away the stone. "Why seek ye the living among the dead?" said he. "He is not here, he is risen as he told you he should do." He then pointed them to the empty sepulchre, and bade them return with the tidings to his disciples.

The Evangelists describe, in the most natural manner, the agitation of the women at this unexpected address. "They went out and fled from the sepulchre; they trembled and were amazed, neither said they anything to any one." Thus they came, breathless and in haste, to the apostles. But so little prepared for such an event were these men, that the words of the women seemed to them like idle tales, and they gave them no credit. None but John and Peter so much as went to examine for themselves; and they, when they found the sepulchre empty, by no means inferred that Jesus was risen, and returned home without further inquiry.

No so Mary Magdalene. She could not persuade herself to withdraw, but remained behind weeping. And she soon had the happiness of seeing and speaking to her risen Master. He came to her from the garden, as she stood in tears before the tomb. At first she did not recognize him, so absorbed was she in her grief. She supposed him to be the gardener, and begged him, if he had removed the body of her Lord, to inform her whither. Jesus uttered her name; the tones of his voice pierced to her heart, and she knew him. "My Master!" she exclaimed;—and it was all she could say. She would have detained him to express her gratitude and joy, but he would not permit her; he told her that for the present he should remain with them; "but go to my brethren," he said, for thus affectionately did he style his disciples, "and say to them, I ascend unto my Father and your Father, and unto my God and your God."

Mary found the eleven still mourning and desponding; and they refused to give credit to her story. They seemed incapable of rising above the stupor and despair in which they had been sunk.

A striking picture of their state of mind on this eventful day is found in the interview which took place in the afternoon, between two disciples, as they were walking to Emmaus, and Jesus himself, who had joined them on the road. He inquired of them the cause of their sadness; and they, supposing him a stranger, gave him the history of Jesus and his death. "But we had trusted," they added, by way of explaining their grief, "that it had been he who should have redeemed Israel." This showed that they still cherished a wrong idea of his redemption; and they repeated the stories which they had heard from the women who had that morning visited the tomb, as things perfectly incredible. Jesus exclaimed against their incredulity, and explained to them from the Scriptures, how the sufferings and resurrection of their Master had been foretold. Still they did not suspect it to be he, until he blessed the bread as they sat down to supper. Then they knew him; and they hastened back to Jerusalem to tell the other disciples.

Here they found that the state of things had somewhat changed. Peter had seen his Lord; and upon his report the eleven had come together, believing and congratulating each other. The two from Emmaus had hardly added their testimony to that of Peter, when Jesus himself entered among them. Their minds were not yet sufficiently composed, and they were startled at his appearance. They doubted if it were not that of a spirit. But he reassured them by allowing

Luke xxiv. 16.

them to feel of his flesh, and convince themselves that it was indeed he. And when they could hardly believe it for joy, as Luke expresses it, he put the matter entirely beyond doubt by asking for food, and eating it in their presence. He remained with them for some time, enlightening their minds, clearing up their doubts, and illustrating the Scriptures which relate to the Messiah. He explained to them the true character of the work to which he had appointed them. He gave them a charge to publish the things of which they had been witnesses, and to preach repentance and remission of sins in his name to all nations; directing them, however, to remain in Jerusalem until they should have fully received power from on high. In this he referred to the effusion of the Spirit, which was to take place fifty days afterward at the feast of Pentecost.

Thus were the minds of the not too credulous apostles put at rest. They were convinced that Jesus had been restored to life, and they began to understand something of the meaning of much in his communications which had formerly been obscure to them. Their minds began to open to the true character of his office, and the grand purposes of his mission. But more than the instructions of an evening were necessary to change their long-established habits of thought, and imbue them thoroughly with the spiritual views which must belong to the preachers of his truth. He therefore continued his interviews with them for forty days. And, as we learn from Paul, he showed himself, not only to the eleven, but to many others, and on one occasion to five hundred at once.

Of these instances, only four are particularly related by the Evangelists; three of which were attended by circumstances of peculiar interest. The first was on the first day of the week succeeding his resurrection. The apostles seem to have commenced at once that practice of meeting on the first day in honor of their Lord, which afterward caused it to be styled "the Lord's day," and to take the place among Christians of the ancient Sabbath. It had happened that on the former evening, when Jesus came to them, Thomas was not with the apostles. He had probably considered the cause so hopeless as to have withdrawn from it altogether. When informed of what had occurred, it seemed to him incredible; and he declared that he could not believe it, except he had the demonstration of his senses; except he could both see and feel the print of the nails and the wound made by the spear. In the succeeding week he was present with the disciples. Jesus again came to them; and, immediately addressing the incredulous apostle, he bade him examine for

Acts i. 3. 1 Cor. xv. 6. John xx. 24.

himself, as he had desired to do. Thomas did so, and was convinced, by the irresistible proof, that there was no delusion, but that his Lord was actually risen.

The next instance is minutely related by John, and presents a scene beautifully characteristic. Peter and some others of the disciples had returned to their residence in Galilee, and had gone upon the lake to fish. Jesus appeared to them on the shore, and took the occasion both to remind Peter of his fault in thrice denying him, and to show that he was fully restored to his confidence. This was an act of delightful consideration. Peter was doubtless suffering deeply from the consciousness of his sin; and, more than this, he not improbably suffered in the good opinion of his companions. It might be said by them, and it was very likely to be said by others, that he who had so basely denied the Saviour ought not to be allowed to take a part in the ministry of his Church. Jesus, therefore, to reinstate him in his own good opinion, and to make evident to all that he was still a trusted friend, drew from him three times a declaration of his devoted attachment; and three times solemnly committed to him the care of his Church. "Simon, son of Jonas, lovest thou me?" "Yea, Lord," was the answer; "thou knowest that I love thee." Jesus rejoined, "Feed

John xxi.

my sheep: feed my lambs." The gratified apostle proved himself worthy of the trust thus kindly reposed in him, by a life of devoted fidelity to the Gospel, and by a martyr's death.

Our Lord once more met his apostles on a mountain in Galilee. There he again assured them of the power and dignity intrusted to him, and bade them go forth, and teach and baptize all nations. It was at this time that he used those words respecting Baptism which have commonly been employed by his ministers in the administration of that rite.

At length the purpose for which he had still lingered upon earth was accomplished. The men to whom his great enterprise was to be intrusted had come at last to understand something of its real nature, and to enter into the spirit with which it should be carried forward. They had begun to exchange their Jewish exclusiveness for their Master's universal philanthropy. They did not, indeed, understand the full glory of his undertaking as he did, nor as they themselves did at a later period. Some remnants of inveterate error still lingered in their minds; so that, even at their last interview with him, one of them asked if he should not yet restore the kingdom to Israel. But they were so far instructed, that they might safely be left without his further personal presence. What

Matthew xxviii. 16.

was yet requisite to their complete illumination would be supplied by the gifts of the Spirit, which he had promised them under the name of "the Comforter." Now therefore he was ready to depart to his Father. He conducted the little band out to Bethany. There, on the eastern summit of Mount of Olivet, he lifted up his hands and blessed them. A cloud received him from their sight, and he ascended up into heaven.

Thus ended the glorious and beneficent ministry of the Son of God among men. Limited to a few persons, confined to a narrow region, continued but for a few months, it laid the foundation of a universal change in the religions of the world, and in the principles and manners of human society. The eleven apostles took up the doctrine which he had committed to them, and went forth to testify to the nations respecting that wonderful person and his wonderful truth. They entered with all their strength upon his great enterprise of reforming the religions and morals of mankind, and carrying the light of immortal truth and hope to all lands and all ages. This purpose had never before entered the mind of man. There was every human probability against its success. Twelve Jews were a small force to be opposed to the religion, the philosophy, and the power of the world. Yet they succeeded; and at the present

Mark xvi. 19. Luke xxiv. 50. Acts i. 9.

day the civilized nations of the earth acknowledge the authority of their crucified Master. He has become, as one of them styled him, "The Prince of the kings of the earth." And the time is plainly approaching, when the whole human race, in all its dwellings, shall bow and worship in his name, and be governed and blessed by the doctrine which he taught in Galilee.

CHAPTER XXIII.

CONCLUSION.

WE have now finished our survey of the history of our Lord's life. It may be well, before closing the work, to give a hasty glance at the main points of the story, and indulge in a few of the thoughts which it naturally suggests.

Let us first transport ourselves back to the age in which he lived. We find that then, owing to certain prophecies in the sacred books of the Jews, there was a strong expectation amongst that people that some remarkable person would soon appear and assume the dominion of the world. They were eagerly looking for him to deliver them from the oppression of the Romans, and restore the nation to its former glory. Under cover of this expectation, we find that many ambitious men came forward, pretended to be the Messiah, collected the people in arms, and rose against the Roman yoke. Such adventurers were eagerly followed; for they were precisely such persons as it was supposed the Messiah would be.

In this state of things, Jesus appears in Galilee

as a teacher and reformer, claiming to bear a special commission from God, and confirming his pretensions by supernatural works. The people gather eagerly around him. They hope that this is the promised deliverer. But he does not declare himself to be such. He simply goes about doing good, and teaching the people. They at length become impatient, and endeavor to compel him by force to be their king. He resists the attempt. He avoids all interference with the civil and political affairs of the country. He preaches peace and non-resistance, repentance and reformation. He denounces hypocrisy, ambition, and all the corruption of the times, and calls men to a pure and more spiritual virtue. The multitude are disappointed. The leading men and the powerful sects are exasperated. They combine against this humble teacher of purity, this bold prophet of truth, and condemn him in their chief council as an impostor and blasphemer. They carry him before the Roman authority as one claiming to be king in opposition to Cæsar. He is put to death by a cruel and ignominious execution, and his panic-stricken followers are dispersed.

Such, in few words, is the history we meet with; and, when thus much has been told us, does it not seem as if the enterprise of Jesus had failed? Could human wisdom give any hope of its revival and success? For who shall be its advocates, when its Head has been cut off, and his friends are scattered in despair? Yet behold, in a few weeks, they reappear, full of confidence and zeal. They speak boldly of their Master; they publicly proclaim him the Messiah; they assert that he has risen from the dead, and given them authority to establish a new dispensation of religion. They are immediately denounced, threatened, and imprisoned; but they adhere manfully to their testimony, they are indefatigable in their zeal, they rapidly gain adherents, and are soon at the head of a powerful and spreading sect, which gains a footing in all the cities of the world, and in three centuries takes the place both of Judaism and Paganism. This is the brief and wonderful history. Who could have anticipated it, that had stood by the infant at Bethlehem? or had seen the young man toiling with Joseph at Nazareth? or had witnessed his death at Calvary, amid insult and derision from Jew and Roman? Who would have dared to conjecture that this person — thus apparently baffled, thwarted, and successfully opposed — was he whom God had appointed to be the chief Reformer and most glorious religious Prince of the world?

We look a little more nearly, and we observe several particulars which corroborate this general impression. The first is, the shortness of the period during which his earthly ministry lasted.

This, as we have seen, did not probably exceed a year and a quarter; certainly not three years and a half. And this little time was spent, not in the capital of the nation, not in securing influence amongst men of learning and power, but almost entirely in the country, and among the peasants of Galilee. He indeed passed from place to place, attended by crowds whom his benefactions and his instructions and the hope of his Messiahship drew about him; but he never announced himself to them as the Messiah, nor took pains to secure their permanent adherence. A few months thus spent would seem to give little promise of a lasting influence; and it is only when we look at the actual result that we are able to conceive it possible that they should have prepared the way for a universal change of religion.

Another similar point is, the small extent of territory to which our Saviour's labors were confined. It does not appear that he visited even the larger part of his own land. He was principally engaged in that small tract which lies between Jerusalem and Capernaum; a distance hardly exceeding eighty miles. And the whole land was but a speck on the face of the earth; being somewhat less in extent than the State of Massachusetts. Yet, upon a small portion of that small spot, Jesus labored for fifteen months, and the consequences have endured to the present day. Eighteen centuries, instead of obliterating, have only served to confirm the impressions which he made, and to extend the work which he began.

The mode which he adopted for establishing his religion and effecting his great purposes is equally worthy of remark. It was altogether by word of mouth, principally in familiar conversation. Even when accompanied by great multitudes, it does not seem to have been his custom to address them in elaborate discourses or systematic lectures. His longest discourse, as recorded by the Evangelists, was not *long;* and in general he was satisfied with a brief illustration of some important truth, or a striking parable which should convey some profitable lesson. What is yet more observable, he committed none of his instructions to writing, nor caused them to be written during his life. The prophets of the Old Testament recorded their prophecies; but Jesus recorded nothing. The illustrious philosophers of antiquity, who hoped to enlighten and benefit mankind, elaborately wrote out their doctrines, that they might remain in a permanent form. But Jesus wrote nothing. He seemed to trust to the Divine energy of the truth itself, and the protecting spirit of God; and cast it abroad, with a sublime unconcern, to make its own way and perpetuate its own existence. And we can account for its preservation and extension only by acknowledging the superintendence of Heaven. Only this could have caused that little seed, so carelessly dropped in Judæa, and so soon forsaken by the Sower, to grow up and become a mighty tree, beneath the shadow of whose branches the nations of the earth are refreshed.

As the circumstances of our Saviour's life thus draw our admiration, so also does his character. This was as wonderful, and as strongly marked by the supernatural, as his miracles. Its opposition to the character which it was expected the Messiah would bear is perfectly marvellous. The Jews looked for a military prince, and he was a religious reformer; they expected a political deliverer, and he refused all connection with their politics; they sought from him the aggrandizement of the nation, and he predicted its overthrow. There was no prominent feature in their description of the Messiah which his character did not contradict. It was not from them therefore, nor from their interpretation of the prophecies, that he drew his notions of the office he claimed. It must have been from another source; and only the consciousness that this was Divine could have encouraged him thus to disappoint and exasperate the people, and rush upon certain death.

How striking does that character appear, when we survey it in the contrast to that corrupt generation! He stood there alone, amongst them, but not of them, nor comprehended by them; meek, pure, benevolent, and spiritual, while those around him were ambitious, sensual, selfish, and worldly; teaching the highest doctrine ever taught, to a people the most opposed to it and the least capable of appreciating it. In this disheartening situation, it is wonderful to observe how his tone of conscious authority was united with the most unassuming gentleness. He appeared with the humility of an ordinary man, yet with a natural air of command. On the most important points of doctrine and of duty, he uttered himself, not as giving an opinion, but as communicating knowledge, and feeling that he had a right to call on men to receive his words. *Ye have heard that it hath been said* thus and thus; but *I say* unto you the contrary. This, we read, excited the astonishment of the people at the time, and it constitutes a feature of his life altogether characteristic.

Yet this consciousness of authority, sustained as it was by supernatural power, never showed itself in arbitrary exercises. On the contrary, there was a singular considerateness and thoughtful kindness both in his instructions and his actions. When he was teaching, nothing is more striking than the tone of gentleness, sweetness, persuasion, which marked his address, — so that the people wondered at his "gracious words." Even his denunciations of the abandoned and hypocritical, stern as they were, were marked with a pathetic and tender solemnity, which made them more affecting than if they had been simply vehement. In his performance of miraculous works the same character is observable. He uniformly selected for them cases of suffering and calamity, in which he could do immediate kindness to men, while establishing his own claims to a Divine original. Any works of power would have effected the latter object; but he chose works of mercy; and thus proved himself to be truly the image of his great Father, whose government perpetually exhibits unlimited Power in union with unbounded Love.

As we thus recapitulate the life and character of our Lord, we feel the proof that he must have come from God. But we must not stop here. We observe the effect which his religion has had on the world, and are still further satisfied. It has not only spread, but it has spread without compulsion and violence, by its own moral power over human minds and wills. It has not only spread, but it has carried blessings with it wherever it has gone. It has overthrown idolatry and superstition, it has reformed the vicious and cheered the penitent. It has been the means of elevating the human race. It has been the encourager of intellectual and moral improvement, the friend of civilization, the advocate and patron of all the best interests of humanity. It has lifted to a higher rank in virtue, intelligence, and happiness that portion of mankind over which it has had sway, than any portion has ever been raised by other means. It is still extending its sway. It is exalting to higher and yet higher perfection those nations which are already Christianized, and it is steadily going on to bring under its influence all the nations of the world. It is proceeding to do what no other power ever ventured to propose to effect, — to banish barbarism and wickedness from the globe, and make civilization and knowledge universal.

The Life of the Saviour is completely narrated, only when we take this wide survey of the consequences to which it is leading; for he still is living in them. His works have not ceased. But we cannot stop even here. The consequences of his labors extend beyond the bounds of this globe. If we would comprehend the value of his life and toils, we must send our thoughts forward into another state of being; we must rise to that higher world which he has peopled and made glorious, must reflect on that eternity in which his innumerable followers are to enjoy infinite and incorruptible bliss. That is a vision which the imagination cannot paint to itself. Eye has not seen, ear has not heard, the heart has not been able to conceive, the joys which are there prepared for those who love God. But to the eye of Faith it is all clear and sure. Life and immortality have been brought to light. And we realize the full wonders of that glory which God has given his Son, only when we connect together in our mind the image of the child at Bethlehem and the sufferer at Calvary with that exalted personage to whom the judgment of the world is committed, and to whom the multitudes that no man can number shall look, with gratitude and thanksgiving, when they render everlasting honors to Him that sitteth on the throne and to the Lamb for ever and ever.

THE END.

Cambridge: Stereotyped and Printed by Welch, Bigelow, & Co.

www.ingramcontent.com/pod-product-compliance
Lightning Source LLC
LaVergne TN
LVHW010228110826
845151LV00004B/1218
9781425526252